Catalogue of permanent circulation coin and paper money types

Volume II

United Kingdom (England and Wales; 1816-2016)

Catalogue of permanent circulation coin and paper money types. Volume II. United Kingdom (England and Wales; 1816-2016)

by H G M Eggenkamp-Vlaanderen

©2016, Dr HGM Eggenkamp-Vlaanderen

ISBN 978-90-816059-8-4 (Soft cover)

Onderzoek & Beleving, Bussum, The Netherlands

post@onderzoek-en-beleving.nl

Catalogue of permanent circulation coin and paper money types

Volume II

United Kingdom (England and Wales; 1816-2016)

H. G. M. Eggenkamp-Vlaanderen

1st edition, 2016

Preface

The period of modern numismatics (since about 1800) is perhaps the most interesting ever. Within this period different types of metallic standards (silver, gold, bimetallic) alternated with periods of fiat currency, and periods of sometimes impressive inflation occurred, in many countries even resulting in hyperinflation. The period after World War II even is the first period in the Earth's history that continued (modest) inflation is the norm in most countries. It also is the period that paper money took over as the main appearance of currency money. This started towards the end of the 19th century when gold coins were for the first time mostly stored in central bank vaults and money started to circulate primarily in the form of banknotes. This became especially important during World Wars I and II when silver and gold coins were hoarded and were replaced by different kinds of paper money in circulation. After World War II circulation gold coins were no longer issued and in most countries even silver coins disappeared from circulation in the years following World War II. As a result, at this moment, coins are solely "small change" in most countries while paper money is used for larger payments. Of course only when payment is made in currency and not taking into account the plastic and even "telephone" money that is increasingly becoming more important. In most countries the trend is that more and more of the payments are done by electronic means, so that the importance of currency for payment has decreased and is expected to continue to decrease considerably in the near future.

In this series of books I aim to classify the different appearances of currency money (both coins and different types of paper and polymer money) in one system. The reason is that I believe it is necessary to look at both appearances to understand the circulation of money in a society. In most current catalogues coins and paper money are treated separately or it is even necessary to acquire different catalogues for coins and for paper money. In fact, the collection of coins and the collection of paper money are very often even considered as different fields of collection and many people either collect coins or collect paper money. However, during the lifetime to a certain denomination coins and paper money series often alternate. For example, in the Netherlands the silver Gulden coin disappeared from circulation in 1914 at the start of World War I, and was replaced by the paper silver certificate with the same value. After the war was over and the situation normalised these paper certificates could be withdrawn. The same happened during World War II, and silver Gulden coins disappeared again, only to be returned to circulation, although in a smaller version, almost 10 years after the war ended. With other words, to understand the circulation of physical money in a country it is necessary to understand how coins and paper money alternate in history.

What I (personally) consider a problem for the collector of circulation coins is the increased issue of different kinds of commemorative coins. Especially after about 1980 the number of commemorative coins in many countries has increased to such an extend that the regular circulation coins, the coins that the public in the street actually uses in commerce, are hardly visible in the major catalogues. It is one of the reasons that I prepared this catalogue and the main reason that only very little information on commemorative coins is provided. They are mentioned if they comply to circulation specification and if they are issued in relatively large quantities at face value. But without images which are provided solely for the regular permanent types.

The currency described in this series is classified according to a newly developed classification scheme. This scheme is built as a hierarchical system based on i) the nominal value, ii) the year a new coin or note series is issued for the first time, iii) the year of issue and iv) if more than one varieties are issued per year an indication of these varieties. In the case that a redenomination or a monetary reform takes place the new currency unit is fit into the old one. For example, the old Franc on France has been replaced by the new Franc, at a ratio cf 100:1, in 1959. As the nominal value in the classification does not change the new Franc will get the same nominal value at the first hierarchical level as the old 100 Franc. This way it is hoped that historical continuity is shown clearly in the series presented in these catalogues.

This series of catalogues has originally been prepared with mainly one collector/numismatist in mind, notably myself. I was already looking for the "ideal" catalogue for a while, and in my opinion it seemed that this was not available. For that reason I decided that I should prepare this catalogue myself. This series, of which this is the second volume and of which hopefully several more will be produced, is the result of this endeavour.

It is hoped that this series of type catalogues will fill the gap that exists for people that are mostly (or even only) interested in circulation coins and paper money, or people that want to learn about the combined history of the currency, both in metal and paper form. They will get an overview of actually used currency in a country, and get a (good) impression of the money the really circulated between the people in a country.

Hans Eggenkamp-Vlaanderen

Introduction to the series

Each volume in this series describes the circulating currency, that is the coins and paper money, that circulate in a certain, more or less defined area. In most volumes this is a single country. Although this may seem vague, the reason is that it is aimed to classify the circulating money in a way that shows the continuity of the money in a region over a longer timespan, mostly from the early 19th century until the present day. In several countries significant political changes happened during this period, and this is generally reflected in the money that has been circulating in that country. Well known examples are countries that were colonised during the 19th century and became independent during the 20th, as well as countries that were occupied for longer or shorter periods during the last two centuries. Also mergers and split-ups of countries are reflected in the circulating currency. An example of colonisation and subsequent independence will be Indonesia, where the coins and notes of the Dutch East Indies will be incorporated as this was the name of Indonesia before its independence. More complex histories are shown in the cases of central Europe (for example Austria-Hungary and its successor states) where significant territorial changes have occurred after World War I and during World War II as well as after the collapse of communist eastern Europe. Examples here are the former Yugoslavia and Russia/former Soviet Union.

Apart from this there are several differences between the major well known catalogues and this catalogue series. It is clearly not a prize catalogue. So at no place indications are given concerning the values of the coins or banknotes. I believe there is no real need to supply values as these are easily findable on various specialised internet sites such as Ebay.com, Catawiki.com and Numista.com. And these values are by definition more up to date than values in a printed catalogue. For the same reason no attempt have been made to discuss the grade of the coins and paper money types. The images presented are not necessary of high quality specimens and sometimes they even are of specimens of only the quality "good" depending on the quality of my personal specimen.

The catalogue aims at presenting a, what I would call, "scientific" classification of the coins and paper money series and types, including a "scientific" way of giving references for each series and type. Although I tried to add images for as many as possible coins and paper money types (at least concerning the "permanent" types) not all of them have been pictured. The reason is that I do not have pictures of all permanent types. Most coins are images from specimens present in my personal collection. 19th century line drawings are taken from contemporary books mostly available from Google books. Bank notes are either scans from my personal collection or obtained from websites from Central Banks after consultation with the relevant division. In some cases even images were made available by the issuing bank. No commemorative coins and banknotes are pictured in this series of catalogues. As written before one of the main reasons for writing this catalogue series is the fact that commemoratives are taking too much space in many modern catalogues and are making the regular circulating coins and notes more and more invisible. Some commemorative series are mentioned however, if the issued numbers are large and if they are issued at face value, so that at least a small chance existed that they were used in commerce. However, no images are supplied. As this catalogue is a "type" catalogue the individual mintage years for coins and years, dates and signature combinations for paper money are not mentioned.

Acknowledgements

I would like to express my gratitude to the Bank of England for giving me permission to reproduce the banknotes that circulated in the United Kingdom. These images have all been taken from their publication

Withdrawn Banknotes Reference Guide that is available from their website (http://www.bankofengland.co.uk/). I would also like to thank my wife, Nina Vlaanderen-Eggenkamp, for her support and patience in writing this catalogue, teaching me how to make photographs of coins and her help in correcting the text of this catalogue.

Table of Contents

The United Kingdom

The United Kingdom is a constitutional monarchy in Northwestern Europe. The country has an area of 242,495 km^2 and an estimated population of 64,716,000 in 2015.

Location of the United Kingdom within Europe (CIA World Factbook)

Map of the United Kingdom showing the main cities (CIA World Factbook)

In this catalogue I will describe the coins and nationwide paper money that have been issued since 1816 in the United Kingdom. In 1816 the so called great recoinage took place, a complete reorganisation of the country's silver and gold coin circulation aimed at stabilising the country's currency after the wars with France (Napoleon) were ended. All coin appearances were considerably modernised during this reorganisation and the country went to a single gold standard with the sovereign coin (the gold one Pound coin) as the base coin. Although they still contained nearly their value in silver (minted at 66 in stead of 62 shillings per troy pound of silver) the silver coins were formally only token coins from this moment and no longer legal tender to any amount, but only for sums of up to 40 shillings (or 2 Pounds).

Paper money was already issued by the Bank of England for some time. At the time of the great recoinage the lowest valued banknotes in circulation were one and two Pounds notes, but these were discontinued after the economy had stabilised and after 1826 the lowest value banknotes in circulation were the 5 Pounds banknotes. As a consequence the paper money described in this catalogue is the paper money that was in circulation in 1816 plus the paper money issued nationwide after that date. This includes the notes issued by the Bank of England, the central bank of the United Kingdom that was established in 1694. It also describes the treasury notes that were issued by the treasury of the United Kingdom during and after World War I (1914-1927). It does not describe the bank notes issued by the seven commercial banks that are still authorised to issue banknotes in Scotland (three of them) and Northern Ireland (four of them). The notes from these banks circulate only in their respective regions, thus not in the whole country, and in England and Wales the Bank of England currently has the monopoly to issue bank notes. For that reason England and Wales are mentioned in the title of this volume, as it strictly speaking describes the money circulating in England and Wales only. In England and Wales private banks also had the right to issue bank notes in the past, but following the Bank Charter Act 1844 this was faded out and the last bank that issued bank notes in England or Wales (Fox, Fowler, and Company) ceased to do so in 1921. As the notes from these provincial banks circulated mostly locally in relatively small amounts they are not incorporated in this catalogue.

Following these restrictions the following coins and notes are incorporated in this catalogue. Circulating coin series issued at face value since 1816, all banknotes issued by the "Bank of England" since about 1816 and treasury notes issued by the treasury of the United Kingdom between 1914 and 1927. This includes the commemorative coins that are issued at face value in large quantities, which are however not depicted in this catalogue (and only briefly mentioned). This indicates that coin series solely consisting of commemorative coins (such as the modern copper-nickel 5 Pounds coins) only have an indication of type and size and the period they are or were issued. Not incorporated are trade coins with nominal values well below their gold or silver contents (such as the Britannia coins), except when these coins have the same specifications as legal value coins that they replaced (so half and one sovereign coins with mintage and issue dates after 1925 will be described). Commemorative coin series issued either at or above face value only in very small mintages are also not mentioned in this catalogue (this includes the recent 20 and 100 Pounds coins that were issued at face value) as their mintages are very small and circulation is also otherwise discouraged by banks and issuing authorities.

In the whole period since 1816 only one currency unit was in use in the United Kingdom. This is the Pound Sterling (ISO code GBP) as it is officially known. However, one important change has happened during this period. In 1971 the Pound Sterling was decimalised. While until 1971 the Pound was divided in 20 shillings of 12 pence each (singular penny) each this was changed to a Pound divided in 100 (decimal) pence from that date. Considering the still relatively large purchasing value of the Pound Sterling in 1971 the change of "shilling" to "5 pence", with other words of the most used coin, was a very large indeed for the general population. As a result of the decimalisation the penny continued to be the smallest regular domination, but its value now was 2.4 times as high. To avoid confusion with the general public between 1971 and 1982 the pence coins were inscribed with "New Penny" or "New Pence". From 1983 this became just "Penny" or "Pence".

In this catalogue only coins and banknotes that were issued (in principle) in the whole country are classified. These are the coins issued by the treasury which have the head the reigning monarch on the obverse. The following kings and queens have reigned the United Kingdom since 1816: George III (coins issued from 1816 until 1820), George IV (issue dates 1821-1830), William IV (issue dates 1831-1837), Victoria (issue dates 1838-1901), Edward VII (issue dates 1902-1910), George V (issue dates 1911-1936), Edward VIII (due to his short reign no coins in his name were issued in the United kingdom, they were however, without his effigy, issued in Fiji, Papua New Guinea, British West Africa and British East Africa), George VI (issue dates 1937-1952) and Elizabeth II (issue dates since 1953). All coins until the present day have the obverse legends in Latin. These legends have changed on a few occasions during the period reported in this catalogue to reflect political changes mostly related to the growth and the later decline of the British empire. This implies for example the addition of the title "IND. IMP." (Emperor/Empress of India) that was added in 1893 and removed after India's independence in 1948, and the removal of the title "BRITT. OMN." that meant "of all the British possessions" after 1953. Paper money that is classified in this catalogue is issued by the treasury of the United Kingdom between 1914 and 1927 and the Bank of England during the whole period since 1816.

Classification system

The classification developed for this book series uses a hierarchical system as described below.

I) The first level is based on the logarithm (base 10) of the nominal values of the coins and paper money that is issued in the country. This is determined by taking the logarithm of the nominal value, add the lowest number to get a positive result, multiply by 10 and put an "O" before. For example the lowest denomination that circulated in the United Kingdom is the half farthing ($^{1}/_{1920}$ GBP or approximately 0.0005), the logarithm is -3.3, to make it positive 4 is added (so that the result is 0.7) then it is multiplied by 10 (so as to get 7) then a leading 0 (zero) and an "O" are added in front and a slash at the end (so that the general code for "half farthing" is "O07/"). In this system the Pound Sterling gets the code "O40/". A redenomination will not change the value. For example, at decimalisation in 1971 the shilling ($^{1}/_{20}$ GBP) coin was replaced with the 5 new pence coin, and both have the same denomination code "O27/". For nominal values that would lead to denomination codes above "O99/" the "O" is replaced by "P", so that the Bank of England one million Pounds notes get the denomination code "P00/".

ii) The second level indicates the actual coin or note series. A coin series is a series of coins issued according to a defined nominal value and well defined technical specifications that include (at least) metal composition, coin shape, weight and diameter. Note series are defined less strict but mostly by the nominal value, the design (a small change indicates a note within the same series, a completely new design defines a new note series) the size and the composition of the note. The series are defined (classified) by the first year that a coin or note series is either minted, authorised or issued. This depends on the information that is readily available. For coin series it is the year that is normally accepted as the first year a coin is officially minted. This is the year that in most catalogues is accepted as the first year of mintage. This is not necessary a year with a high mintage. For note series this is the year that the note is first issued. This year is not normally printed on the note for modern Bank of England notes. In this catalogue these dates are taken from the "Withdrawn Banknotes Reference Guide" that is available from the Bank of England website. After the year either a "C" or an "N" is added to indicate if the series is a coin or a note series. In those cases that more than one series was issued or authorised in the same year a superscript "1" or "2" etc. is added.

iii) The third level indicates the year that an individual coin or note is minted or issued as indicated on the note or coin. For coins this is the mintage year as indicated on the coin. For notes the system is necessarily more complicated. Older, white, banknotes from the Bank of England were dated when they were issued, and in theory every date could appear on a note. Modern bank notes, as well as the treasury notes, are not dated. For that reason at this level the year that a new signature appeared on the notes is used at this leel. For Bank of England bank notes that is the year that a new Chief Cashier was appointed, for treasury notes the year a new Secretary of the Treasury was appointed.

iv) At the final level the variability with a coin or note series is indicated. For standard circulation coins this exists of a capital letter for each of the common obverse and reverse sides. A big change in the design is indicated by a different letter, small variations in the design by a superscript number. Different issues of the same obverse/reverse combination in a year (such as the appearance of a mint mark when coins were not minted at the Royal Mint but at one of the private mints in Birmingham) are indicated by small letters after the design indications. Commemorative coins are indicated with a "Z" at this level. When more commemoratives are issued in one year it is followed by a superscript number. If either the obverse or the reverse of a commemorative coin is of a standard design this is indicated at this level too, as is for example shown in modern 50 pence and 2 Pounds coins, which in most cases have a regular obverse. In this catalogue however no commemorative designs are described at it is a "permanent types" only catalogue.

Set-up of the catalogue

In the following pages the coins and paper money series that circulated in the United Kingdom are presented. Starting from the lowest nominal value (the half farthing) until highest printed value (the 100 million Bank of England banknote). Within each nominal value a short summary is given of all series (either coins or notes) that were issued and an indication is given of the periods that a certain nominal value was circulating in the country. After this introduction a table is presented that shows the various coin and note series, including the years these were issued, their compositions and the mass, the diameter and the thickness of the specimens. In the case of paper money series only the size is given. No attempts have been made to show the weight or the thickness of the paper money series. This table gives a good impression how coin and paper money series alternated for each nominal value.

Then a section is written for each coin or paper money series. For each coin series after the title an image shows the exact size of the coin. As paper money normally has a size that is larger than the size of a page in this book for paper money this is not given. This figure is followed by images and short descriptions of the obverse and reverse types. Coins are all presented at the same size (1 inch, 2.54 cm), paper money is presented at a width of 1.8 inch or 4.57 cm, while the height depends on the actual width to height ratio of the note. Finally a table is presented that indicates the various coin or paper money types (possible obverse-reverse combinations) and the years that these combinations were issued. In the case of coins cross references are given with the major world coin catalogues (KM#, Standard Catalog of World Coins by CL Krause and C Mischler; S#, Weltmunzkatalog 19. Jahrhundert by G Schön und H Kahn, and 20. und 21. Jahrhundert by G Schön und G. Schön and Y#, A Catalog of Modern World Coins 1850-1964 by RS Yeoman). In the case of paper money a cross reference is given with the P# from the

Standard Catalog of World Paper Money by A Pick (3rd edition 1980) or N Shafer and GS Cuhaj (9th edition 2003, 16th edition 2010). Finally an empty column with "X" in the heading is presented in which the colletor can indicate whether a specimen of the coin or paper money type is present in his or her own collection. The presence of commemorative coins in the coin series is roughly mentioned with the years they were issued, but no further descriptions are given.

The catalogue

1. O07/ Half farthing ($^1/_{1920}$ GBP)

The half farthing can be considered as the smallest coin that ever circulated in the United Kingdom. Originally this coin was minted for use in Ceylon only as the purchasing value was considered as too small to be useful in Britain. It was made legal tender in Britain in 1842 (in Ceylon already in 1828) and demonetised in 1869 after the changeover from copper to bronze coins. Although "British" coins with lower values than a half farthing do exist (the third and the quarter farthing) these were never legal tender in Britain (the third farthing in Malta only and the quarter farthing in Ceylon only) and for that reason they are not described in this volume of the catalogue.

This denomination was issued as only one series containing of pure copper coins.

Series	Years	Comp.	Mass (g)	Size (mm)	THK (mm)
O07/1828C	1828-1856	100% Cu	2.4	18	1.0

1.1. O07/1828C Copper half farthing (1828-1856)

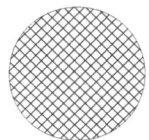

One permanent obverse design for each of the three monarchs that featured this coin, two reverse designs, the second of which was redesigned when it became legal tender in Britain to reflect this change in status.

Obverse A

Obverse C

Obverse A: Head of King George IV facing left.

Obverse B: Head of King William IV facing right.

Obverse C: Young head of Queen Victoria facing left.

Reverse A

Reverse B¹

Reverse B²

Reverse A: Seated Britannia facing right with shield and trident.

Reverse B¹: Crown above "HALF FARTHING" above rose with three leaves.

Reverse B²: As reverse B¹ but rose now with thistle and shamrock (representing Scotland and Ireland).

Type	Years	KM#	S#	Y#	X
O07/1828CyyyyAA	1828-1830	704	C16		
O07/1828CyyyyBA	1837	724	C18		
O07/1828CyyyyCB¹	1839	738	90	C2	
O07/1828CyyyyCB²	1842-1856	738	90	C2	

2. O10/ Farthing ($^1/_{960}$ GBP)

Traditionally the farthing was the smallest coin circulating in the United Kingdom. It got is name from the fact that during the middle ages silver pennies were devided into four things to be able to give small change. Since the great recoinage officially two series of farthings have been issued. A pure copper until 1860 and a bronze between 1860 and 1956 when it was discontinued. However, due to ghosting problems with the bronze coins (although this was more prominent with pennies and half pennies) the bronze composition was changed during in 1923. During World War II the bronze composition was changed again, but now to save tin that was needed for war efforts. Each of these three bronze compositions are considered different series for the purpose of this catalogue, even it is is very difficult (or impossible) to observe the differences between the three series without sophisticated equipment.

Series	Years	Comp.	Mass (g)	Size (mm)	THK (mm)
O10/1821C	1821-1864	Copper (100% Cu)	4.8	22	1.4
O10/1860C	1860-1922	Bronze (95% Cu, 1% Zn, 4% Sn)	2.835	20	1.0
O10/1923C	1923-1956	Bronze (95.5% Cu, 1.5% Zn, 3% Sn)	2.835	20	1.0
O10/1942C	1942-1945	Bronze (97% Cu, 2.5% Zn, 0.5% Sn)	2.835	20	1.0

2.1. O10/1821C Copper farthing (1821-1864)

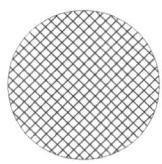

Four obverse types. Two reverse types, the last of which has two subtypes.

Obverse A

Obverse B

Obverse C

Obverse D

Obverse A: Laureate head of King George IV facing left.

Obverse B: Bare head of King George IV facing left. Image from Christmas (1864).

Obverse C: Head of King William IV facing right.

Obverse D: Young head of Queen Victoria facing left.

Obverse A

Obverse B¹

Obverse B²

Reverse A: Britannia facing right with date below.

Reverse B¹: Britannia facing right with rose, shamrock and thistle below. "REX" in legend (for "king").

Reverse B²: As reverse B¹ but "REG" in legend (for "queen").

As with all 19th century copper and bronze coins several minor design variations are found.

Type	Years	KM#	S#	Y#	X
O10/1821CyyyyAA	1821-1826	677	53		
O10/1826CyyyyBB[1]	1826-1830	697	54		
O10/1826CyyyyCB[1]	1831-1837	705	76		
O10/1826CyyyyDB[2]	1838-1864	725	91	1	

2.2. O10/1860C 1st bronze farthing (1860-1923)

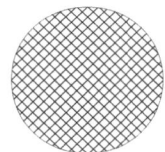

Four obverse designs, the first of which, the "bun head" of Queen Victoria consists of two versions indicating the ageing of the queen. Two reverse designs, all showing Britannia facing right, but heavily redesigned in 1895. The low-tide variety of 1903 is not considered here as a separate subdesign. The height of the tide on bronze coins seems to be quite variable depending on the die, and depends in my opinion on the die cutter and is not an official design characteristic. As with all 19th century copper and bronze coins several minor design variations are found, and for detailed information on this variety several specialised books can (and should) be consulted (e.g. Peck, 1964; Freeman, 1985 or Couby, 1986, 2005).

Obverse A¹   *Obverse A²*   *Obverse A³*

Obverse B   *Obverse C*   *Obverse D*

Obverse A¹: "Bun head" of Queen Victoria facing left. Beaded border.

Obverse A²: As obverse A¹ with toothed border.

Obverse A³: Slightly aged "Bun head" of Queen Victoria.

Obverse B: Veiled head of Queen Victoria facing left

Obverse C: Head of King Edward VII facing right.

Obverse D: Head of King George V facing left.

Reverse A¹   *Reverse A²*   *Reverse B*

Reverse A¹: Britannia facing right with ship to the right and lighthouse to the left. Beaded border.

Reverse A²: As reverse A¹ with toothed border.

Reverse B: Britannia facing right with ship and lighthouse removed.

Type	Years	KM#	S#	Y#	X
O10/1860CyyyyA^{1}A^1	1860	747.1	116	16	
O10/1860CyyyyA^{2}A^2	1860-1873	747.2	116, 117	16	
O10/1860CyyyyA^{3}A^2	1874-1895	753	116, 117	16	
O10/1860CyyyyBB	1895-1901	788	136	32	
O10/1860CyyyyCB	1902-1910	792	281	46	
O10/1860CyyyyDB	1911-1923	808	297	60	

2.3. O10/1923C 2nd bronze farthing (1923-1956)

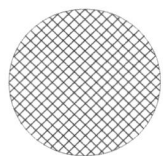

The exact date of the change from the first to the second bronze composition is not very clear. Both the Coincraft catalogue (Lobel, 1996) and Tony Clayton's website (www.coins-of-the-uk.co.uk) only discuss the bronze composition of the penny. For the penny the situation is clear as this coin was not minted during the changeover to another bronze composition. Both Perkins (2013) and Schön (2014) indicate that the changeover for farthings and halfpennies was in 1923, and that year is taken as the start year for the current catalogue.

No change in design was observed when the bronze composition changed, so the first design of this series is exactly the same as the last design of the previous series. Except a few years during World War II when a very low tin composition was used this series lasted until the demonetisation of this denomination. In 1956 the last farthing was minted and it was finally demonetised in 1960.

Obverse A¹   *Obverse A²*   *Obverse B¹*

Obverse B²   *Obverse C¹*   *Obverse C²*

Obverse A¹: Head of King George V facing left, this is the same design (obverse D) as used for O10/1860C. Initials "B.M." with stops.

Obverse A²: So called "modified effigy", initials "BM" without stops and larger teeth along the rim.

Obverse B¹: Head of King George VI with "IND IMP" in legend.

Obverse B²: As obverse B¹ with "IND IMP" removed.

Obverse C¹: Head of Queen Elizabeth II facing right with "BRITT OMN" in legend.

Obverse C²: As obverse C¹ with "BRITT OMN" removed.

Reverse A¹   *Reverse A²*   *Reverse B*

Reverse A¹: Britannia facing right.

Reverse A²: As reverse A¹ but sharper struck and with larger teeth along the rim.

Reverse B: Wren.

Type	Years	KM#	S#	Y#	X
O10/1923CyyyyA^{1}A^1	1923-1925	808	297	60	
O10/1923CyyyyA^{2}A^2	1926-1936	825	297	60	
O10/1923CyyyyB^{1}B	1937-1948*	846	334	82	
O10/1923CyyyyB^{2}B	1949-1952	867	353	1C4	
O10/1923CyyyyC^{1}B	1953	881	367	116	
O10/1923CyyyyC^{2}B	1954-1956	895	385	127	

*From 1942-1945 issued in different bronze alloy (see O10/1942C)

2.4. O10/1942C 3rd bronze farthing (1942-1945)

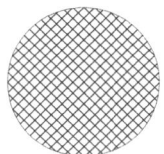

During World War II a bronze alloy with even less tin was used to save this metal for war efforts. Towards the end of the war the coin reverted back to the pre-war composition. Only one obverse and reverse design, that is equal to O10/1923CyyyyB^{1}B.

Obverse   *Reverse*

Obverse: Head of King George VI facing right.

Reverse: Wren.

Type	Years	KM#	S#	Y#	X
O10/1942Cyyyy	1942-1945	843	334	82	

3. O13/ Halfpenny ($^1/_{480}$ GBP)

The origin of the halfpenny is comparable to that of the farthing as during medieval times it was produced by cutting a silver penny in two halves. Only later (round) silver halfpennies were produced. Copper halfpennies were fir the first time introduced during the reign of King Charles II in the second half of the 17th century. Since the great recoinage officially two series of halfpennies have been issued. A pure copper until 1860 and a bronze between 1860 and 1967 when it was discontinued due to the decimalisation. Due to ghosting problems with the bronze coins the bronze composition was changed during 1923. Again during World War II the bronze composition was changed again, but now to save tin that was needed for war efforts. In 1945 the halfpenny composition was reverted back to its pre-war composition. From 1959 it was again minted in the very low tin alloy, this time to save money due to the diminishing purchasing value of the halfpenny. Each of these three bronze compositions are considered different series for the purpose of this catalogue, even it is is very difficult (or impossible) to observe the differences between the three series without sophisticated equipment.

Series	Years	Comp.	Mass (g)	Size (mm)	THK (mm)
O13/1825C	1825-1860	Copper (100% Cu)	9.3	28	1.7
O13/1860C	1860-1922	Bronze (95% Cu, 1% Zn, 4% Sn)	5.67	25	1.3
O13/1923C	1923-1956	Bronze (95.5% Cu, 1.5% Zn, 3% Sn)	5.67	25	1.3
O13/1942C	1942-1970	Bronze (97% Cu, 2.5% Zn, 0.5% Sn)	5.67	25	1.3

3.1. O13/1825C Copper halfpenny (1825-1860)

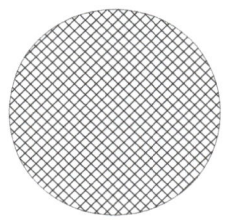

Three obverse designs (one per monarch) and one reverse design, which has two subdesigns depending on the sex of the monarch.

Obverse A   *Obverse C*

Obverse A: Head of King George IV facing left.

Obverse B: Head of King William IV facing right.

Obverse C: Young head of Queen Victoria facing left.

19

Reverse A¹　　　　　*Reverse A²*

Reverse A¹: Britannia facing right with rose, shamrock and thistle below. "REX" in legend (for "king").

Reverse A²: As reverse A¹ but "REG" in legend (for "queen").

As with all 19th century copper and bronze coins several minor design variations are found.

Type	Years	KM#	S#	Y#	X
O13/1825CyyyyAA¹	1825-1827	692	55		
O13/1825CyyyyBA¹	1831-1837	706	77		
O13/1825CyyyyCA²	1838-1860	726	92	2	

3.2. O13/1860C 1ˢᵗ bronze halfpenny (1860-1922)

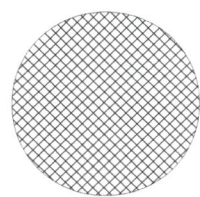

Four obverse designs, the first of which, the "bun head" of Queen Victoria consists of four versions that indicate the ageing of the queen. Two reverse designs, both showing Britannia facing right, but heavily redesigned in 1895.

Obverse A²

Obverse A⁴

Obverse B

Obverse C

Obverse D

Obverse A¹: "Bun head" of Queen Victoria facing left. Wears rose at her necklace. Beaded border.

Obverse A²: As obverse A¹ with toothed border.

Obverse A³: Slightly aged "Bun head" of Queen Victoria. Wears rose at her necklace.

Obverse A⁴: Even more aged head of Queen Victoria. Wears brooch at her necklace.

Obverse B: Veiled head of Queen Victoria facing left.

Obverse C: Head of King Edward VII facing right.

Obverse D: Head of King George V facing left.

Reverse A²

Reverse B

Reverse A¹: Britannia facing right with ship to the right and lighthouse to the left. Beaded border.

Reverse A²: As reverse A¹ with toothed border.

Reverse B: Britannia facing right, ship and lighthouse

removed.

As with all 19th century copper and bronze coins several minor design variations are found.

Type	Years	KM#	S#	Y#	X
O13/1860CyyyyA^{1}A^1	1860	748.1	118	17	
O13/1860CyyyyA^{2}A^2	1860-1874	748.2	118, 119	17	
O13/1860CyyyyA^{3}A^2	1874-1883	754	118, 119	17	
O13/1860CyyyyA^{4}A^2	1883-1894	754	118	17	
O13/1860CyyyyBB	1895-1901	789	137	33	
O13/1860CyyyyCB	1902-1910	793	282	47	
O13/1860CyyyyDB	1911-1922	809	298	61	

3.3. O13/1923C 2nd bronze halfpenny (1923-1958)

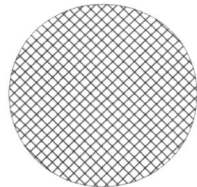

The exact date of the change from the first to the second bronze composition is not very clear. Both the Coincraft catalogue (Lobel, 1996) and Tony Clayton's website (www.coins-of-the-uk.co.uk) only discuss the composition of the penny. For the penny the situation is clear as this coin was not minted during the changeover to a different bronze composition. Both Perkins (2013) and Schön (2014) indicate that the changeover for farthings and halfpennies was in 1923, and that year is taken as the start year for the current catalogue.

No change in design was observed when the bronze composition changed, so the first design of this series is exactly the same as the last design of the previous series.

Obverse A¹ *Obverse A²* *Obverse A³*

Obverse B¹ *Obverse B²* *Obverse C¹*

Obverse C²

Obverse A¹: Head of King George V facing left, "B.M." on truncation.

Obverse A²: As obverse A¹ but "BM" without stops.

Obverse A³: Smaller and more sharply struck head of King George V.

Obverse B¹: Head of King George VI with "IND IMP" in legend.

Obverse B²: As obverse B¹ with "IND IMP" removed.

Obverse C¹: Head of Queen Elizabeth II facing right with "BRITT OMN" in legend.

Obverse C²: As obverse C¹ with "BRITT OMN" removed.

| *Reverse A¹* | *Reverse A²* | *Reverse B* |

Reverse A¹: Britannia facing right.

Reverse A²: As reverse A¹ but redesigned and sharper struck.

Reverse B: The ship "Golden Hind" of Sir Francis Drake.

Type	Years	KM#	S#	Y#	X
O13/1923CyyyyA¹A¹	1923-1925	809	298	61	
O13/1923CyyyyA²A²	1925-1927	824	298	61	
O13/1923CyyyyA³A²	1928-1936	837	312	62	
O13/1923CyyyyB¹B	1937-1948*	844	335	83	
O13/1923CyyyyB²B	1949-1952	868	354	105	
O13/1923CyyyyC¹B	1953	882	368	117	
O13/1923CyyyyC²B	1954-1958	896	386	128	

*From 1942-1945 issued in a different bronze alloy (see O13/1942C).

3.4. O13/1942C 3ʳᵈ bronze halfpenny (1942-1970)

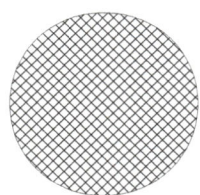

During World War II a bronze alloy with even less tin was used to save this metal for war efforts. Towards the end of the war the mint reverted to the pre-war composition. In 1959 again this alloy started to be used for halfpennies (and later pennies) as a matter to save on the cost of tin. This series is known with two designs, which are equal to O13/1923CyyyyB¹B and O13/1923CyyyyC²B. The halfpenny was last minted in 1968 with the date of 1967 and demonetised on 1ˢᵗ August 1969. It was incorporated in the farewell proof set of 1970, although halfpennies with the date of 1970 were never legal tender.

Obverse A　　　　*Obverse B*　　　　*Reverse A*

Obverse A: Head of King George VI facing left.

Obverse B: Head of Queen Elizabeth II facing right.

Reverse A: The ship "Golden Hind" of Sir Francis Drake.

Type	Years	KM#	S#	Y#	X
O13/1942CyyyyAA	1942-1945	844	335	83	
O13/1942CyyyyBA	1959-1970	896	386	128	

4. O16/ Penny ($^{1}/_{240}$ GBP)

As long as England exists the penny is the base coin of its monetary system. Originally made of silver, the currency penny was first changed to copper in the cartwheel issue of 1797. In 1860 the copper penny gave way to a bronze version. The silver penny continued to be minted as "Maundy" penny distributed by (or on behalf of) the British Monarch during the Maundy Thursday ceremony. Maundy money consists of the four smallest silver coins that were originally in circulation (1, 2, 3 and 4 pence). The Maundy ceremony developed from the original washing of the feet by Jesus the day before his execution and developed to a ceremony in which the monarch performed an act of benevolence towards the poor. Maundy money as such started in the reign of Charles II with an undated issue of hammered coins in 1662. The coins were a four penny, three penny, two penny and one penny piece but it was not until 1670 that a dated set of all four coins appeared. Prior to this, ordinary coinage was used for Maundy gifts, silver pennies alone being used by the Tudors and Stuarts for the ceremony. Currently still poor people are given these coins in the ceremony on Maundy Thursday. The number is related to the age of the monarch, as as many poor men and women as the age of the monarch receive as many pence as the age of the monarch. Thus the total issue increases with the age of the reigning monarch. Although the mintage of the silver penny for this purpose has always been very small it was actually used as currency by the recipients as they were poor people that could really use the money. Only in 1947 when the silver money was changed to copper-nickel and when the Maundy money reverted back to sterling silver the connection with real circulating money was broken. As the Maundy money was minted with a currency design it is incorporated here. Both the copper/bronze and the silver penny regularly changed their composition. As a result four series of silver pennies and four series of copper/bronze pennies have been issued between 1816 and 1970. In 1971 all Maundy pennies where revalued to 1 new penny and coins from 1971 on are classified as new pennies (GBP 0.01, O20/).

Series	Years	Comp.	Mass (g)	Size (mm)	THK (mm)
O16/1817C	1817-1970	Silver (92.5% Ag, 7.5% Cu)	0.4713	11	0.5
O16/1825C	1825-1860	Copper (100% Cu)	18.8	34	2.3
O16/1860C	1860-1922	Bronze (95% Cu, 1% Zn, 4% Sn)	9.45	30.81	1.4
O16/1921C	1921-1922	Silver (50% Ag, 40% Cu, 10% Ni)	0.4713	11	0.5

Series	Years	Comp.	Mass (g)	Size (mm)	THK (mm)
O16/1923C	1923-1927	Silver (50% Ag, 50% Cu)	0.4713	11	0.5
O16/1926C	1926-1954	Bronze (95.5% Cu, 1.5% Zn, 3.5% Sn)	9.45	30.81	1.4
O16/1928C	1928-1946	Silver (50% Ag, 40% Cu, 5% Zn, 5% Ni)	0.4713	11	0.5
O16/1944C	1944-1970	Bronze (97% Cu, 2.5% Zn, 0.5% Sn)	9.45	30.81	1.4

4.1. O16/1817C Sterling silver penny (1817-1970)

By the time of the great recoinage the silver penny had developed into Maundy money only. For that reason its mintage numbers are very small in all years of mintage. It is included here because the designs followed those of the earlier currency pennies and never commemorative designs were adapted. The composition of the Maundy coins followed the composition of the other silver coins until silver was abolished from the coinage. At that moment the Maundy coins reverted back to sterling silver. That explains the gap between 1920 and 1946 in this series.

Obverse A

Obverse B

Obverse D

Obverse F   *Obverse G*

Obverse A: Head of King George III facing right. Image from Bonneville (1849).

Obverse B: Head of King George IV facing left. Image from Bonneville (1849).

Obverse C: Head of King William IV facing right.

Obverse D: Young head of Queen Victoria facing left.

Obverse E: "Jubilee" head of Queen Victoria facing left.

Obverse F: Veiled head of Queen Victoria facing left.

Obverse G: Head of King Edward VII facing right.

Obverse H: Head of King George V facing left.

Obverse I¹: Head of King George VI facing left with "IND IMP" in legend.

Obverse I²: As obverse B¹ with "IND IMP" removed.

Obverse J¹: Head of Queen Elizabeth II facing right with "BRITT OMN" in legend.

Obverse J²: As obverse C¹ with "BRITT OMN" removed.

Reverse A   *Reverse B¹*   *Reverse B²*

Reverse A: Crowned "1", no date. Image from Bonneville (1849).

Reverse B¹: Crowned "1" between divided date with wreath around.

Reverse B²: As reverse B¹ with different (imperial) crown.

Type	Years	KM#	S#	Y#	X
O16/1817CyyyyAA	1817-1820	668	45.1		
O16/1817CyyyyBB[1]	1822-1830	683	57.1		
O16/1817CyyyyCB[1]	1831-1837	708	80.1		
O16/1817CyyyyDB[1]	1838-1887	727	95.1	A12	
O16/1817CyyyyEB[2]	1888-1892	770	122.1	A27	
O16/1817CyyyyFB[2]	1893-1901	775	139.1	A41	
O16/1817CyyyyGB[2]	1902-1910	795	284	A55	
O16/1817CyyyyHB[2]	1911-1920	811	300	A81	
O16/1817CyyyyI[1]B[2]	1947-1948	846a	349a	A93	
O16/1817CyyyyI[2]B[2]	1949-1952	870	362	A113	
O16/1817CyyyyJ[1]B[2]	1953	884	381	A126	
O16/1817CyyyyJ[2]B[2]	1954-1970	898	395	A135	

4.2. O16/1825C Copper penny (1825-1860)

Three obverse designs (one per monarch) and one reverse design, with two subdesigns depending on the sex of the monarch.

Obverse A

Obverse B

Obverse C

Obverse A: Head of King George IV facing left.

Obverse B: Head of King William IV facing right. Image from Christmas (1864).

Obverse C: Young head of Queen Victoria facing left.

Reverse A¹   *Reverse A²*

Reverse A¹: Britannia facing right with rose, shamrock and thistle below. "REX" in legend (for "king").

Reverse A²: As reverse A¹ but "REG" in legend (for "queen").

As with all 19th century copper and bronze coins several minor design variations are found.

Type	Years	KM#	S#	Y#	X
O16/1825CyyyyAA¹	1825-1827	693	56		
O16/1825CyyyyBA¹	1831-1837	707	78		
O16/1825CyyyyCA²	1841-1860	739	93	3	

4.3. O16/1860C 1ˢᵗ bronze penny (1860-1922)

Four obverse designs, the first of which, the "bun head" of Queen Victoria consists of two versions showing the ageing of the queen. Two reverse designs, both showing

Britannia facing right, but heavily redesigned in 1895. As with all 19th century copper and bronze coins many minor design variations are found. Some of these are quite famous, such as the various reverses with different tide heights (1897, 1902). The differences are however small and for the purpose of this classification only the 1895 penny with a larger distance between trident and legend then the later coins is given a separate subdesign. The effigy of King George V was designed in such a way that it caused considerable ghosting on the reverse of the coin. The reason that caused this ghosting was that its relief was too high and as a result bronze was drawn from the reverse to fill the obverse. This initiated research to change the alloy in order to prevent this ghosting. This resulted in the 2nd bronze penny in 1926 and is also the reason that no bronze pennies with mintage years 1923, 1924 and 1925 were produced.

Obverse A²   *Obverse A³*   *Obverse B*

Obverse C   *Obverse D*

Obverse A¹: "Bun head" of Queen Victoria facing left with beaded border

Obverse A²: As obverse A¹ with toothed border.

Obverse A³: Slightly aged "Bun head" of Queen Victoria.

Obverse B: Veiled head of Queen Victoria facing left.

Obverse C: Head of King Edward VII facing right.

Obverse D: Head of King George V facing left.

Reverse A²   *Reverse B²*

Reverse A: Britannia facing right with ship to the right and lighthouse to the left.

Reverse B^1: Britannia facing right with ship and lighthouse removed. Distance between trident and "P" of "PENNY" 2 mm.

Reverse B^2: Like reverse B^1 but distance between trident and "P" of "PENNY" 1 mm.

As with all 19th century copper and bronze coins several minor design variations are found.

Type	Years	KM#	S#	Y#	X
O16/1860CyyyyA¹A¹	1860	749.1	120	18	
O16/1860CyyyyA²A²	1860-1874	749.2	120, 121	18	
O16/1860CyyyyA³A²	1874-1894*	755	120, 121	18	
O16/1860CyyyyBB¹	1895	790	138	34	
O16/1860CyyyyBB²	1895-1901	790	138	34	
O16/1860CyyyyCB²	1902-1910	794	283	48	
O16/1860CyyyyDB²	1911-1922	810	299	63	

*According to Perkins (2014) portrait aged (further?) in 1881. Consult specialised literature for details!

4.4. O16/1921C 1ˢᵗ 50% silver penny (1921-1922)

Due to rapidly increasing silver prices in 1920 it was decided to decrease the silver content in all silver coins to from 92.5% to 50%. Unfortunately the base metal part of the coins toned unattractive and for that reason experiments were done with different base metal compositions until in 1927 a final composition was decided upon. The coins produced in each of these compositions are considered different coin series for the purpose of this catalogue, although there are no design changes.

Obverse: Head of King George V facing left.

Reverse: Crowned "1" between divided date with wreath around.

Type	Years	KM#	S#	Y#	X
O16/1921Cyyyy	1921-1922	811a	300a	E81	

4.5. O16/1923C 2ⁿᵈ 50% silver penny (1923-1927)

In 1923 the base metal content of the Maundy coins changed. No changes were observed in the designs.

Obverse: Head of King George V facing left.

Reverse: Crowned "1" between divided date with wreath around.

Type	Years	KM#	S#	Y#	X
O16/1923Cyyyy	1923-1927	811a	300a	E81	

4.6. O16/1926C 2nd bronze penny (1926-1954)

Due to excessive ghosting in George V pennies mintage was halted in 1922 and it was expected that a different bronze alloy would solve the problem. In 1926 mintage started again with the original obverse and this was later that year replaced with the modified effigy. Only after the smaller head was introduced in 1928 the ghosting problem was solved. During World War II the penny was minted for a few years with the very low tin alloy to save this metal for war efforts (see O16/1944C).

| Obverse A¹ | Obverse A² | Obverse A³ |

| Obverse B¹ | Obverse B² | Obverse C¹ |

Obverse A¹: Head of King George V facing left, "B.M." on truncation.

Obverse A²: As obverse A¹ but "BM" without stops.

Obverse A³: Smaller and more sharply struck head of King George V.

Obverse B¹: Head of King George VI with "IND IMP" in legend.

Obverse B²: As obverse B¹ with "IND IMP" removed.

Obverse C¹: Head of Queen Elizabeth II facing right with "BRITT OMN" in legend.

Obverse C²: As obverse C¹ with "BRITT OMN" removed.

Reverse A¹

Reverse A²

Reverse B¹

Reverse B²

Reverse A¹: Britannia facing right.

Reverse A²: As reverse A¹ but redesigned and sharper struck.

Reverse B¹: Heavily redesigned Britannia with lighthouse to the left. Toothed border.

Reverse B²: As reverse B¹ with beaded border.

Type	Years	KM#	S#	Y#	X
O16/1926CyyyyA¹A¹	1926	810	299	63	
O16/1926CyyyyA²A¹	1926	826	299	63	
O16/1926CyyyyA²A²	1927	826	299	63	
O16/1926CyyyyA³A²	1928-1936	838	313	64	

Type	Years	KM#	S#	Y#	X
O16/1926CyyyyB¹B¹	1937-1948*	845	336	84	
O16/1926CyyyyB²B¹	1949-1952	869	355	106	
O16/1926CyyyyC¹B²	1953	883	369	118	
O16/1926CyyyyC²B²	1954**	897	387	A128	

*From 1942-1945 issued in different bronze alloy (see O16/1944C).

**Only two specimens are known of this coin (Perkins, 2014). Same designs as O16/1944CyyyyBA².

4.7. O16/1928C 3ʳᵈ 50% silver penny (1928-1946)

The last change in the base metal composition of the 50% silver coins took place at the moment that the coinage under George V was modernised in 1927/1928. The first Maundy coins in this alloy were issued in 1928 and this alloy continued to be in use until the removal of silver altogether from the general circulating coinage. At that moment the Maundy coins reverted back to sterling (925‰) silver.

Obverse A: Head of King George V facing left.

Obverse B: Head of King George VI facing left.

Reverse A: Crowned "1" between divided date with wreath around.

Type	Years	KM#	S#	Y#	X
O16/1928CyyyyAA	1928-1936	839	300a	E81	
O16/1926CyyyyBA	1937-1946	846	349	A93	

4.8. O16/1944C 3rd bronze penny (1944-1970)

During World War II this bronze allow was used to save tin for the war efforts, during the reign of Queen Elizabeth II to save money on the production of the very large amounts of pennies that were needed to be minted during the last years of its existence. This coin was demonetised after the decimalisation of the currency on 15 February 1971 and officially withdrawn from circulation on 31 August 1971.

Obverse A   *Obverse B*

Obverse A: Head of King George VI facing left.

Obverse B: Head of Queen Elizabeth facing right.

Reverse A¹   *Reverse A²*

Revere A¹: Britannia facing right with lighthouse at the left. Toothed border.

Reverse A²: As reverse A¹ with beaded border.

Type	Years	KM#	S#	Y#	X
O16/1944CyyyyAA¹	1944-1945	845	336	84	
O16/1944CyyyyBA²	1961-1970	897	387	A128	

5. O17/ Half (new) penny (GBP 0.00½)

Although its nominal value is larger than the old penny this small coin was the lowest valued coin that was introduced during decimalisation. Already during its introduction it was expected that it would only have a relatively short lifetime and indeed inflation made the coin redundant and it was demonetised in December 1984. Only one series was produced during the short lifetime of this coin.

Series	Years	Comp.	Mass (g)	Size (mm)	THK (mm)
O17/1971C	1971-1984	Bronze (97% Cu, 2.5% Zn, 0.5% Sn)	1.78	17.14	0.9

5.1. O17/1971C Bronze half (new) penny (1971-1984)

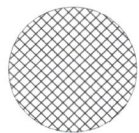

Issued with one obverse and one reverse design. The reverse design changed slightly when, in 1982 the name of the "new penny" became simply "penny" as by that time confusion between the old and the new pennies was no longer a risk.

Obverse A   *Reverse A¹*   *Reverse A²*

Obverse A: Head of Queen Elizabeth II facing right.

Reverse A¹: Crown with "½" below. "NEW PENNY" above.

Reverse A²: As reverse A¹, but "HALF PENNY" above.

Type	Years	KM#	S#	Y#	X
O17/1971CyyyyAA¹	1971-1981	914	401		
O17/1971CyyyyAA²	1982-1984	926	417		

6. O19/ Twopence ($^1/_{120}$ GBP)

The overwhelming majority of pre-decimal twopences issued after the great recoinage were Maundy twopence coins. Only in three years, 1838, 1843 and 1848 larger amounts were minted for use in British Guyana and the West Indies. As these coins were of the same design as the Maundy coins they were legal tender in Great Britain. It is not known if (many) of these currency twopences were returned to England to be used in commerce. These series follow exactly the series of the 1 penny Maundy coins and four series can be recognised, one in sterling silver and three considerably shorter runs in 50% silver.

Series	Years	Comp.	Mass (g)	Size (mm)	THK (mm)
O19/1817C	1817-1970	Silver (92.5% Ag, 7.5% Cu)	0.9426	13	0.7
O16/1921C	1921-1922	Silver (50% Ag, 40% Cu, 10% Ni)	0.9426	13	0.7
O16/1923C	1923-1927	Silver (50% Ag, 50% Cu)	0.9426	13	0.7
O16/1928C	1928-1946	Silver (50% Ag, 40% Cu, 5% Zn, 5% Ni)	0.9426	13	0.7

6.1. O19/1817C Sterling silver twopence (1817-1970)

The silver twopence is included here for the same reasons as the silver penny. Interestingly in three years currency issues were minted for use in the West Indies as stated above. All other years have, like the silver penny, very small mintage figures. The composition of the Maundy coins followed the composition of the other silver coins until silver was abolished from the coinage. At that moment the Maundy coins reverted back to starling silver. This explains the gap between 1920 and 1946 in this series.

Obverse A

Obverse B

Obverse C

Obverse D   *Obverse E*   *Obverse J²*

Obverse A: Head of King George III facing right. Image from Bonneville (1849).

Obverse B: Head of King George IV facing left. Image from Bonneville (1849).

Obverse C: Head of King William IV facing right. Image from Bonneville (1849).

Obverse D: Young head of Queen Victoria facing left.

Obverse E: "Jubilee" head of Queen Victoria facing left.

Obverse F: Veiled head of Queen Victoria facing left.

Obverse G: Head of King Edward VII facing right.

Obverse H: Head of King George V facing left.

Obverse I¹: Head of King George VI facing left with "IND IMP" in legend.

Obverse I²: As obverse B¹ with "IND IMP" removed.

Obverse J¹: Head of Queen Elizabeth II facing right with "BRITT OMN" in legend.

Obverse J²: As obverse C¹ with "BRITT OMN" removed.

Reverse A   *Reverse B¹*   *Reverse B²*

Reverse A: Crowned "2", no date. Image from Bonneville (1849).

Reverse B¹: Crowned "2" between divided date with wreath around.

Reverse B²: As reverse B¹ with different (imperial) crown.

Type	Years	KM#	S#	Y#	X
O19/1817CyyyyAA	1817-1820	669	45.2		
O19/1817CyyyyBB¹	1822-1830	684	57.2		
O19/1817CyyyyCB¹	1831-1837	709	80.2		
O19/1817CyyyyDB¹	1838-1887	771	95.2	B12	
O19/1817CyyyyEB²	1888-1892	776	139.2	B41	
O19/1817CyyyyFB²	1893-1901	776	139.2	B41	
O19/1817CyyyyGB²	1902-1910	796	285	B55	
O19/1817CyyyyHB²	1911-1920	812	301	B81	
O19/1817CyyyyI¹B²	1947-1948	847a	350a	B93	
O19/1817CyyyyI²B²	1949-1952	871	363	B113	
O19/1817CyyyyJ¹B²	1953	885	382	B126	
O19/1817CyyyyJ²B²	1954-1970	899	396	B135	

6.2. O19/1921C 1ˢᵗ 50% silver twopence (1921-1922)

Same design as O19/1817CyyyyHB².

Obverse: Head of King George V facing left.

Reverse: Crowned "2" between divided date with wreath around.

Type	Years	KM#	S#	Y#	X
O19/1921Cyyyy	1921-1922	812a	301a	F81	

6.3. O16/1923C 2nd 50% silver twopence (1923-1927)

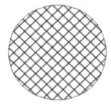

Same design as O19/1817CyyyyHB[2].

Obverse: Head of King George V facing left.

Reverse: Crowned "2" between divided date with wreath around.

Type	Years	KM#	S#	Y#	X
O19/1923Cyyyy	1923-1927	812a	301a	F81	

6.4. O19/1928C 3rd 50% silver twopence (1928-1946)

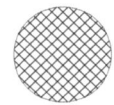

The last change in the base metal composition of the 50% silver coins took place at the moment that the coinage under George V was modernised in 1927/1928. The first Maundy coins in this alloy were issued in 1928 and this alloy continued to be in use until the removal of silver altogether from the general coinage.

Obverse B   *Reverse A*

Obverse A: Head of King George V facing left.

Obverse B: Head of King George VI facing left.

Reverse A: Crowned "2" between divided date with wreath around.

Type	Years	KM#	S#	Y#	X
O19/1928CyyyyAA	1928-1936	840	301a	F81	
O19/1926CyyyyBA	1937-1946	847	350a	B93	

7. O20/ (New) penny (GBP 0.01)

The (new) penny coin (1/100 of a Pound) was first introduced (together with the ½ and 2 pence coins) in a wallet in 1968 that also contained the new 5 and 10 pence coins. These last coins were legal tender from the start, having the same characteristics as the old 1 and 2 shilling coins, the bronze coins were dated 1971 and would only be legal tender from decimal day on 15 February 1971. Two series of currency pennies have been issued. Originally this coin was issued in bronze, and since 1992 in copper plated steel. Also the Maundy penny continued to be issued each year. There was no change whatsoever with this coin, but from 1971 it was revalued to 1 new penny and for that reason decimal Maundy pennies are placed under the decimal penny heading (O20/).

Series	Years	Comp.	Mass (g)	Size (mm)	THK (mm)
O20/1971C[1]	1971-1999	Bronze (97% Cu, 2.5% Zn, 0.5% Sn)	3.564	20.32	1.52
O20/1971C[2]	1971-....	Silver (92.5%	0.4713	11	0.5

44

Series	Years	Comp.	Mass (g)	Size (mm)	THK (mm)
		Ag, 7.5% Cu)			
O20/1992C	1992-....	Copper plated steel (94% steel [Fe, C, Mn] with 6% Cu plating)	3.564	20.32	1.65

7.1. O20/1971C¹ Bronze (new) penny (1971-1999)

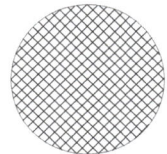

Issued with three obverse designs and one reverse design. The reverse design was changed slightly in 1982 by replacing the word "NEW" with "ONE".

Obverse A   *Obverse B*   *Obverse C*

Obverse A: Second head of Queen Elizabeth II facing right.

Obverse B: Third head of Queen Elizabeth II facing right.

Obverse C: Fourth head of Queen Elizabeth II facing right.

Reverse A¹   *Reverse A²*

Reverse A¹: Crowned portcullis with "1" below. "NEW PENNY" in legend above.

Reverse A²: As reverse A¹ but legend "ONE PENNY".

Type	Years	KM#	S#	Y#	X
O20/1971C¹yyyyAA¹	1971-1981	915	402		
O20/1971C¹yyyyAA²	1982-1984	927	417		
O20/1971C¹yyyyBA²	1985-1992	935	425		
O20/1971C¹yyyyCA²	1999	986a	479		

7.2. O20/1971C² Maundy penny (1971-....)

Continuation of the earlier Maundy penny with no change in design or specification, but revalued from "old" to "new" pence.

Obverse: First head of Queen Elizabeth II facing right.

Reverse: Crowned "1" between divided date with wreath around.

Type	Years	KM#	S#	Y#	X
O20/1971Cyyyy	1971-...	898	395	A135	

7.3. O20/1992C Copper plated steel penny (1992-....)

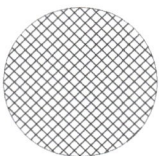

Since 1992 the penny has been produced as a copper plated coin to save on its production costs. No change in design was made during the changeover. Only in 1999 the penny that was incorporated in the sets produced for collectors has once more been made in the old bronze composition. Three obverse design (the second with two versions) and two reverse designs.

Obverse A

Obverse B¹

Obverse B²

Obverse C

Obverse A: Third head of Queen Elizabeth II facing right.

Obverse B¹: Fourth head of Queen Elizabeth II facing right with beads along the border.

Obverse B¹: As obverse B¹ but without beads.

Obverse C: Fifth head of Queen Elizabeth II facing right.

Reverse A   *Reverse B*

Reverse A: Crowned portcullis with "1" below. "ONE PENNY" in legend above.

Reverse B: Centre left part of shield of the royal arms.

Type	Years	KM#	S#	Y#	X
O20/1992CyyyyAA	1992-1997	935a	425a		
O20/1992CyyyyB¹A	1998-2008	986	479a		
O20/1992CyyyyB²B	2008-2015	1107	594		
O20/1992CyyyyCB	2015-....				

8. O21/ Threepence ($^{1}/_{80}$ GBP)

Around the time of the great recoinage the threepence was solely used as silver coin for the Maundy ceremony. In 1834 production of larger amounts of this coin started for use in Ceylon and the West Indies, together with 1½ pence coins. The 1½ pence coins never became legal tender in the United Kingdom and for that reason are omitted from this catalogue. However, the threepences, being also issued as Maundy money were legal tender in the United Kingdom. From 1845 the threepence was also minted for use in the United Kingdom. Starting in 1927 two versions of the silver threepence were issued, one as general currency with a different design while the classic "crowned 3" design continued to be used as Maundy money. Due to its small size the silver coins were not popular especially in England and were largely replaced by large nickel-brass coins from 1937. The silver coins were more popular in Scotland and the West Indies and they continued to be produced until 1944/1945. Interestingly a copper-nickel threepence was incorporated in the coinage act of 1946, but it was never minted.

Series	Years	Comp.	Mass (g)	Size (mm)	THK (mm)
O21/1817C	1817-1970	Silver (92.5% Ag, 7.5% Cu)	1.4138	16	0.7
O21/1920C	1920-1922	Silver (50% Ag, 40% Cu, 10% Ni)	1.4138	16	0.7
O21/1921C	1921	Silver (50% Ag, 45% Cu, 5% Mn)	1.4138	16	0.7
O21/1922C	1922-1926	Silver (50% Ag, 50% Cu)	1.4138	16	0.7
O21/1927C	1927-1946	Silver (50% Ag, 40% Cu, 5% Zn, 5% Ni)	1.4138	16	0.7
O21/1937C	1937-1970	Nickel-brass (79% Cu, 20% Zn, 1% Ni)	6.8	21 (sides), 22 (corners)	2.5

8.1. O21/1817C Sterling silver threepence (1817-1970)

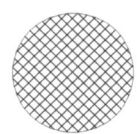

Used as Maundy money only from 1817 until 1833 and from 1947 until 1970. Issued for use in the West Indies only from 1834 until 1844. A total of 10 obverse and two reverse types have been used.

Obverse A *Obverse B²* *Obverse C*

Obverse D *Obverse E* *Obverse F*

Obverse G *Obverse H*

Obverse A: Head of King George III facing right. Image from Bonneville (1849).

Obverse B¹: Head of King George IV facing left. The head of the king is smaller than usual due to the use of the punch of the twopence as the original one for the threepence was broken, and could not be replaced in time for the Maundy ceremony.

Obverse B²: Normal sized head of King George IV facing left. Image from Bonneville (1849).

Obverse C: Head of King William IV facing right. Image from Bonneville (1849).

Obverse D: Young head of Queen Victoria facing left.

Obverse E: "Jubilee" head of Queen Victoria facing left.

Obverse F: Veiled head of Queen Victoria facing left.

Obverse G: Head of King Edward VII facing right.

Obverse H: Head of King George V facing left.

Obverse I¹: Head of King George VI facing left with "IND IMP" in legend.

Obverse I²: As obverse B¹ with "IND IMP" removed.

Obverse J¹: Head of Queen Elizabeth II facing right with "BRITT OMN" in legend.

Obverse J²: As obverse C¹ with "BRITT OMN" removed.

Reverse A

Reverse B¹

Reverse B²

Reverse A: Crowned "3", no date. Image from Bonneville (1849).

Reverse B¹: Crowned "3" between divided date with wreath around.

Reverse B²: As reverse B¹ but different (imperial) crown.

Type	Years	KM#	S#	Y#	X
O21/1817CyyyyAA	1817-1820	670	45.3		
O21/1817CyyyyB¹B¹	1822	685.1	57.3		
O21/1817CyyyyB²B¹	1823-1830	685.2	57.3		
O21/1817CyyyyCB¹	1831-1837	710	80.3, 81		
O21/1817CyyyyDB¹	1838-1887	730	95.3, 97	A3, C12	
O21/1817CyyyyEB²	1888-1892	758	122.3, 123	A18, C27	
O21/1817CyyyyFB²	1893-1901	777	139.3, 140	35, C41	
O21/1817CyyyyGB²	1902-1910	797	286	49, C55	
O21/1817CyyyyHB²	1911-1920	813	302	65, C81	

Type	Years	KM#	S#	Y#	X
O21/1817CyyyyI¹B²	1947-1948	850a	351a	C93	
O21/1817CyyyyI²B²	1949-1952	872	364	C113	
O21/1817CyyyyJ¹B²	1953	887	383	C126	
O21/1817CyyyyJ²B²	1954-1970	901	397	C135	

8.2. O21/1920C 1st 50% silver threepence (1920-1922)

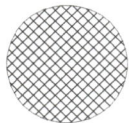

Same design as O21/1817CyyyyHB².

Obverse *Reverse*

Obverse: Head of King George V facing left.

Reverse: Crowned "3" between divided date with wreath around.

Type	Years	KM#	S#	Y#	X
O21/1920Cyyyy	1920-1922	813a	302a	65, G81	

8.3. O21/1921C 2nd 50% silver threepence (1921)

In 1921 tests were also made with a 50% silver that contains some manganese in stead of nickel. Apparently these tests were not successful and the composition was reverted back to the nickel containing silver. The threepences in this (very short) series are undistinguishable from the former and have the same design as O21/1817CyyyyHB².

Obverse　　　　　　*Reverse*

Obverse: Head of King George V facing left.

Reverse: Crowned "3" between divided date with wreath around.

Type	Years	KM#	S#	Y#	X
O21/1921Cyyyy	1921	813a	302a	65	

8.4. O21/1922C 3ʳᵈ 50% silver threepence (1922-1927)

Initially the same design as O21/1817CyyyyHB². Part of the 1926 coins featured the "modified" effigy of King George V, while the Maundy coin used the original effigy. Due to size and wear the two obverses for the 1926 coins are very difficult to tell apart.

Obverse A¹　　　　*Obverse A²*　　　　*Reverse A*

Obverse A[1]: Head of King George V facing left.

Obverse A[2]: "Modified" effigy of King George V facing left.

Reverse A: Crowned "3" between divided date with wreath around.

Type	Years	KM#	S#	Y#	X
O21/1922CyyyyA¹A	1922-1927	813a	302a	65, G81	
O21/1922CyyyyA²A	1926	827	302a	65	

8.5. O21/19278C 4ᵗʰ 50% silver threepence (1927-1946)

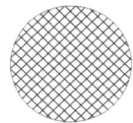

The last change in the base metal composition of the 50% silver coins took place at the moment that the coinage under George V was modernised in 1927. In 1927 a new obverse design was introduced for the non-Maundy coins, while the reverse of the Maundy coins remained the same. This zinc and nickel containing alloy continued to be in use until the abolishment of silver currency threepences in 1945. Since 1942 these coins were in fact only minted for use in the West Indies. Maundy threepences continued to be minted in 50% silver until 1946, after which they were minted in sterling silver again (see O21/1817C).

Obverse A   *Obverse B²*

Obverse A: Head of King George V facing left.

Obverse B¹: Head of King George VI facing left, with "F D IND IMP" in legend.

54

Obverse B²: As obverse B¹ but without "F D IND IMP" in legend.

Reverse A   *Reverse C*

Reverse A: Three oak-sprigs with acorns.

Reverse B: Crowned "3" between divided date with wreath around (Maundy reverse).

Reverse C: Shield with rose behind.

Type	Years	KM#	S#	Y#	X
O21/1927CyyyyAA	1927-1936	831	314	70	
O21/1927CyyyyAB	1928-1936	827	302a	G81	
O21/1927CyyyyB¹B	1937-1946	850	351	C93	
O21/1927CyyyyB²C	1937-1946	848	338	86	

8.6. O21/1937C Nickel-brass threepence (1937-1970)

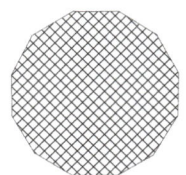

As the silver threepence was, especially in England, considered too small a coin for general circulation work was done during the reign of King Edward VIII to develop a larger, clearly distinguishable threepence coin. The result was the distinctive, fairly thick, 12 sided coin made of nickel-brass. This coin continued to be in circulation until decimal day, and it was finally withdrawn from circulation on 31 August 1971. Two obverses each with two versions and two reverses were in use between 1937 and 1971.

Obverse A¹

Obverse A²

Obverse B¹

Obverse B²

Obverse A¹: Head of King George VI facing left with "IND IMP" in legend.

Obverse A²: As obverse B¹ with "IND IMP" removed.

Obverse B¹: Head of Queen Elizabeth II facing right with "BRITT OMN" in legend.

Obverse B²: As obverse C¹ with "BRITT OMN" removed.

Reverse A

Reverse B

Reverse A: Thrift plant.

Reverse B: Crowned portcullis with chains. This design has in part been used for the later decimal penny that only has a slightly smaller value.

Type	Years	KM#	S#	Y#	X
O21/1937CyyyyA¹A	1937-1948	849	337	85	

Type	Years	KM#	S#	Y#	X
O21/1937CyyyyA^2A	1949-1952	873	356	107	
O21/1937CyyyyB^1B	1953	886	370	119	
O21/1937CyyyyB^2B	1954-1970	900	388	129	

9. O22/ Fourpence ($^1/_{60}$ GBP)

The fourpence shows for a large part the same characteristics as the twopence. During the whole period since the great recoinage it was in fact used as Maundy money only. Only between 1836 and 1862 a fourpence coin was in general use in the United Kingdom, and this had different characteristics than the Maundy type coin (smaller and thicker), although it was of the same weight. As a result four Maundy series and one non-Maundy series of fourpences have been issued between 1816 and 1970.

Series	Years	Comp.	Mass (g)	Size (mm)	THK (mm)
O22/1817C	1817-1970	Silver (92.5% Ag, 7.5% Cu)	1.885	18	0.7
O22/1836C	1836-1888	Silver (92.5% Ag, 7.5% Cu)	1.885	16	0.9
O22/1921C	1921-1922	Silver (50% Ag, 40% Cu, 10% Ni)	1.885	18	0.7
O16/1923C	1923-1927	Silver (50% Ag, 50% Cu)	1.885	18	0.7
O16/1928C	1928-1946	Silver (50% Ag, 40% Cu, 5% Zn, 5% Ni)	1.885	18	0.7

9.1. O22/1817C Sterling silver maundy fourpence (1817-1970)

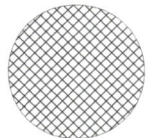

The silver fourpence is included here for the same reasons as the other Maundy coins. It was always minted in very small numbers. The composition of the Maundy coins followed the composition of the other silver coins until silver was abolished from the coinage. At that moment the Maundy coins reverted back to starling silver. This explains the gap between 1920 and 1946 in this series.

Obverse A | Obverse B | Obverse C

Obverse D | Obverse E | Obverse F

Obverse A: Head of King George III facing right. Image from Bonneville (1849).

Obverse B: Head of King George IV facing left. Image from Bonneville (1849).

Obverse C: Head of King William IV facing right.

Obverse D: Young head of Queen Victoria facing left. Image from Homans & Mushet (1872).

Obverse E: "Jubilee" head of Queen Victoria facing left.

Obverse F: Veiled head of Queen Victoria facing left.

Obverse G: Head of King Edward VII facing right.

Obverse H: Head of King George V facing left.

Obverse I¹: Head of King George VI facing left with "IND IMP" in legend.

Obverse I²: As obverse B¹ with "IND IMP" removed.

Obverse J¹: Head of Queen Elizabeth II facing right with "BRITT OMN" in legend.

Obverse J²: As obverse C¹ with "BRITT OMN" removed.

Reverse A   *Reverse B¹*   *Reverse B²*

Reverse A: Crowned "4", no date. Image from Bonneville (1849).

Reverse B¹: Crowned "4" between divided date with wreath around.

Reverse B²: As reverse B¹ but different (imperial) crown.

Type	Years	KM#	S#	Y#	X
O22/1817CyyyyAA	1817-1820	671	45.4		
O22/1817CyyyyBB¹	1822-1830	686	57.4		
O22/1817CyyyyCB¹	1831-1837	711	80.4		
O22/1817CyyyyDB¹	1838-1887	732	95.4	D12	
O22/1817CyyyyEB²	1888-1892	773	122.4	D27	
O22/1817CyyyyFB²	1893-1901	778	139.4	D41	
O22/1817CyyyyGB²	1902-1910	798	287	D55	
O22/1817CyyyyHB²	1911-1920	814	303	D81	
O22/1817CyyyyI¹B²	1947-1948	851a	352a	D93	

Type	Years	KM#	S#	Y#	X
O22/1817CyyyyI²B²	1949-1952	874	365	D113	
O22/1817CyyyyJ¹B²	1953	888	384	D126	
O22/1817CyyyyJ²B²	1954-1970	902	398	D135	

9.2. O22/1836C Fourpence groat (1836-1888)

The non-Maundy fourpence was issued both in the colonies in the West Indies and in Great Britain in 1836. It is said that it was introduced due to lobby work from MP Joseph Hume as a convenient way to pay the London cab fare. The coin was however not popular by the London cab drivers as before the introduction of this coin often a sixpence was offered without demanding the twopence change, so in many cases they lost their tip. This coin has the same weight and metal content as the fourpence Maundy coin, but it was slightly smaller and thus thicker than that coin. It lost its popularity quickly after the reintroduction of the silver threepence in British currency in 1845 as it has the same size of this coin and could easily be confused. After 1845 it was mainly issued for the West Indies and the last issue from 1888 was solely issued in these colonies. The coin is issued with three obverse designs and one reverse design.

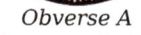
Obverse A

Obverse B

Reverse A

Obverse A: Head of King William IV facing right. Image

from Bonneville (1849).

Obverse B: Young head of Queen Victoria facing right.

Obverse C: Jubilee head of Queen Victoria facing right.

Reverse A: Britannia.

Type	Years	KM#	S#	Y#	X
O22/1836CyyyyAA	1836-1837	723	82		
O22/1836CyyyyBA	1838-1862	731	97A(?)	4	
O22/1836CyyyyCA	1888	772	124	B2	

9.3. O22/1921C 1st 50% silver fourpence (1921-1922)

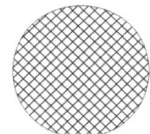

Same design as O22/1817CyyyyHB.

Obverse: Head of King George V facing left.

Reverse: Crowned "4" between divided date with wreath around.

Type	Years	KM#	S#	Y#	X
O22/1921Cyyyy	1921-1922	814a	303a	H31	

9.4. O22/1923C 2nd 50% silver fourpence (1923-1927)

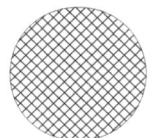

Same design as O22/1817CyyyyHB.

Obverse: Head of King George V facing left.

Reverse: Crowned "4" between divided date with wreath

around.

Type	Years	KM#	S#	Y#	X
O22/1923Cyyyy	1923-1927	814a	303a	H81	

9.5. O22/1928C 3rd 50% silver fourpence - (1928-1946)

The last change in the base metal composition of the 50% silver coins took place at the moment that the coinage under George V was modernised in 1927/1928. The first Maundy coins in this alloy were issued in 1928 and this alloy continued to be in use until the removal of silver altogether from the general coinage.

Obverse A: Head of King George V facing left.

Obverse B: Head of King George VI facing left.

Reverse A: Crowned "4" between divided date with wreath around.

Type	Years	KM#	S#	Y#	X
O22/1928CyyyyAA	1928-1936	841	303a	H81	
O22/1928CyyyyBA	1937-1946	851	352	D93	

10. O23/ 2 (new) pence (GBP 0.02)

The 2 (new) pence coin was first introduced (together with the ½ and 1 penny coins) in a wallet in 1968 that also contained the new 5 and 10 pence coins. It is legal tender since decimal day on 15 February 1971. Two series of currency two pence coins have been issued. Originally this coin was issued in bronze, and since 1992 in copper plated steel. Also the Maundy twopence continued to be issued each year. There was no change whatsoever with this coin, but from 1971 it was revalued to 2 new pence and for that reason decimal Maundy twopences are under this heading.

Series	Years	Comp.	Mass (g)	Size (mm)	THK (mm)
O23/1971C[1]	1971-1999	Bronze (97% Cu, 2.5% Zn, 0.5% Sn)	7.12	25.9	1.85
O23/1971C[2]	1971-....	Silver (92.5% Ag, 7.5% Cu)	0.9426	13	0.7
O23/1992C	1992-....	Copper plated steel (94% steel [Fe, C, Mn] with 6% Cu plating)	7.12	25.9	2.03

10.1. O23/1971C[1] Bronze 2 (new) pence (1971-1999)

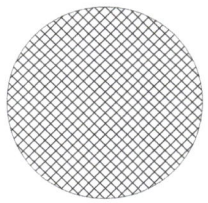

Issued with three obverse designs and one reverse design. The reverse design was changed slightly in 1982 by replacing the word "NEW" with "TWO".

Obverse A *Obverse B* *Obverse C*

Obverse A: Second head of Queen Elizabeth II facing right.

63

Obverse B: Third head of Queen Elizabeth II facing right.

Obverse C: Fourth head of Queen Elizabeth II facing right.

Reverse A¹   *Reverse A²*

Reverse A^1: Plumes within coronet with "2" below. "NEW PENCE" in legend above.

Reverse A^2: As reverse A^1 but legend "TWO PENCE".

Type	Years	KM#	S#	Y#	X
O23/1971C¹yyyyAA¹	1971-1981	916	403		
O20/1971C¹yyyyAA²	1982-1984	928	418		
O23/1971C¹yyyyBA²	1985-1992	936	426		
O23/1971C¹yyyyCA²	1998-1999	987a	480		

10.2. O23/1971C² Maundy twopence (1971-....)

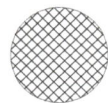

Continuation of the earlier Maundy twopence with no change in design or specification, but revalued from "old" to "new" pence.

Obverse: First head of Queen Elizabeth II facing right.

Reverse: Crowned "2" between divided date with wreath around.

Type	Years	KM#	S#	Y#	X
O23/1971C²yyyy	1971-...	899	396	B135	

10.3. O23/1992C Copper plated steel 2 pence (1992-....)

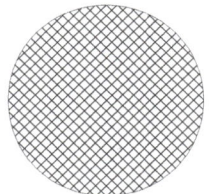

Since 1992 the 2 pence coin has been produced as a copper plated coin to save on its production costs. No change in design was made during the changeover. In 1998 the currency 2 pence coin was produced both in bronze and in copper plated steel. In 1999 the two pence coin penny that was incorporated in the sets produced for collectors was made of bronze. Three obverse design (the second with two versions) and two reverse designs.

Obverse A

Obverse B¹

Obverse B²

Obverse C

Obverse A: Third head of Queen Elizabeth II facing right.

Obverse B¹: Fourth head of Queen Elizabeth II facing right with beads along the border.

Obverse B²: As obverse B¹ but without beads.

Obverse C: Fifth head of Queen Elizabeth II facing right.

Reverse A   *Reverse B*

Reverse A: Plumes within coronet with "2" below. "TWO PENCE" in legend above.

Reverse B: Upper right part of shield of the royal arms.

Type	Years	KM#	S#	Y#	X
O23/1992CyyyyAA	1992-1997	936a	426a		
O23/1992CyyyyB¹A	1998-2008	987	480a		
O23/1992CyyyyB²B	2008-2015	1108	595		
O23/1992CyyyyCB	2015-....				

11. O24/ Sixpence (GBP 0.02½)

The sixpence (½ shilling) is one of the classic English denominations and it has been issued since the time of King Edward VI (about 1550). Since the recoinage it was a sterling silver coin, debased to 50% in 1920 and to copper-nickel in 1947. Although no decimal coin replaced the sixpence it was only demonetised on 30 June 1980 as the coin was extensively used in London Underground ticket machines. After decimal day these coins were valid for 2½ new penny. A total of six coin series can be determined, four of which consist of 50% silver coins with different base metal compositions.

Series	Years	Comp.	Mass (g)	Size (mm)	THK (mm)
O24/1816C	1816-1920	Silver (92.5% Ag, 7.5% Cu)	2.835	19	1.0
O24/1920C	1920-1922	Silver (50% Ag, 40% Cu, 10%	2.835	19	1.0

Series	Years	Comp.	Mass (g)	Size (mm)	THK (mm)
		Ni)			
O24/1921C	1921	Silver (50% Ag, 45% Cu, 5% Mn)	2.835	19	1.0
O24/1922C	1922-1927	Silver (50% Ag, 50% Cu)	2.835	19	1.0
O24/1927C	1927-1946	Silver (50% Ag, 40% Cu, 5% Zn, 5% Ni)	2.835	19	1.0
O24/1947C	1947-1970	Copper-nickel (75% Cu, 25% Ni)	2.835	19	1.1

11.1. O24/1816C Sterling silver sixpence (1816-1920)

As this coin was issued for almost 100 years the number of obverse and reverse design is rather large. A total of 9 obverse and 7 reverse design can be recognised. One obverse and one reverse design also show several (smaller) variations.

Obverse A

Obverse B

Obverse C

Obverse D

Obverse E¹

Obverse E²

Obverse E³

Obverse F

Obverse G

Obverse H

Obverse I

Obverse A: Head of King George III facing right.

Obverse B: Laureate head of King George IV facing left. Image from Bonneville (1849).

Obverse C: Bare head of King George IV facing left.

Obverse D: Head of King William IV facing right.

Obverse E¹: Young head of Queen Victoria facing left. Image from Bonneville (1849).

Obverse E²: As obverse E¹ but lower relief.

Obverse E³: As obverse E¹ but slightly aged.

Obverse F: Jubilee head of Queen Victoria facing left.

Obverse G: Veiled head of Queen Victoria facing left.

Obverse H: Head of King Edward VI facing right.

Obverse I: Head of King George V facing left.

Reverse A

Reverse B

Reverse C

Reverse D

Reverse E¹

Reverse E²

Reverse E³

Reverse E⁴

Reverse G

Reverse A: Crowned shield within Garter.

Reverse B: Garnished shield with large crown. Image from Bonneville (1849).

Reverse C: Crowned shield within Garter, more square shield than reverse A. Image from Bonneville (1849).

Reverse D: Lion on crown.

Reverse E¹: Crowned "SIX PENCE" with wreath around.

Reverse E²: As reverse E¹ with die number above date.

Reverse E³: As reverse E¹ with "SIX PENCE" larger.

Reverse E⁴: As reverse E³ with different (imperial) crown.

Reverse F: Crowned shield within Garter (like the reverse

of the 1887 shilling). Different from reverse C in removal of Hanover shield, different crown and different age. This design was quickly removed as it was too similar in design and size as the half-sovereign and could be passed off as such easily after gold plating.

Reverse G: Lion on (imperial) crown with value below.

Type	Years	KM#	S#	Y#	X
O24/1816CyyyyAA	1816-1820	665	46		
O24/1816CyyyyBB	1821	678	58		
O24/1816CyyyyBC	1824-1826	691	62		
O24/1816CyyyyCD	1826-1829	698	65		
O24/1816CyyyyDE^1	1831-1837	712	83		
O24/1816CyyyyE^{1}E^1	1838-1863	733.1	98	5	
O24/1816CyyyyE^{1}E^2	1864-1866	733.2	99	5	
O24/1816CyyyyE^{2}E^2	1867-1879	751.1	99	5	
O24/1816CyyyyE^{2}E^1	1871-1880	751.2	100	5	
O24/1816CyyyyE^{3}E^1	1880-1883	757	100	5	
O24/1816CyyyyE^{3}E^3	1884-1887	757	100	5	
O24/1816CyyyyFF	1887	759	125	19	
O24/1816CyyyyFE^4	1887-1893	760	126	22	
O24/1816CyyyyGE^4	1893-1901	779	141	36	
O24/1816CyyyyHE^4	1902-1910	799	288	50	
O24/1816CyyyyIG	1911-1920	815	304	66	

11.2. O24/1920C 1st 50% silver sixpence (1920-1922)

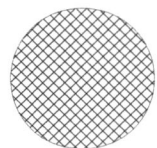

Due to rapidly increasing silver prices in 1920 it was decided to decrease the silver content in all silver coins from 92.5% to 50%. As the base metal part of the coins toned unattractively experiments were done with different base metal compositions until in 1927 a final composition was decided upon. The coins produced in each of these compositions are considered different coin series for the purpose of this catalogue, although there were no design changes. Same design as O24/1816CyyyyIG.

Obverse   *Reverse*

Obverse: Head of King George V facing left.

Reverse: Lion on (imperial) crown with value below.

Type	Years	KM#	S#	Y#	X
O24/1920Cyyyy	1920-1922	815a	304a	66	

11.3. O24/1921C 2ⁿᵈ 50% silver sixpence (1921)

In 1921 experiments were also done with a 50% silver containing some manganese in stead of nickel. Apparently these experiments were not successful and the composition was revered back to the nickel containing silver. The sixpences in this series are undistinguishable from the former, the have the same design as O24/1816CyyyyIG.

Obverse: Head of King George V facing left.

Reverse: Lion on (imperial) crown with value below.

Type	Years	KM#	S#	Y#	X
O24/1921Cyyyy	1921	815a	304a	66	

11.4. O24/1922C 3rd 50% silver sixpence (1922-1926)

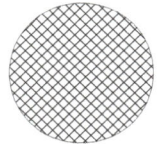

Initially the same design as O24/1816CyyyyIG. However in 1926 the "modified" effigy of King George V started to be used. As these effigies are very similar, due to the small size of these coins and and the wear it generally obtained in circulation the two obverses for the 1926 coins are very difficult to tell apart.

Obverse A¹   *Obverse A²*   *Reverse A*

Obverse A¹: Head of King George V facing left. The signature of the designer as "B.M." more or less in the middle of the truncation of the King's neck.

Obverse A²: Modified effigy of King George V, signature of designer as "BM" with no stops and more to the right of the truncation of the King's neck.

Reverse A: Lion on (imperial) crown with value below.

Type	Years	KM#	S#	Y#	X
O241922CyyyyA¹A	1922-1926	815a	304a	66	
O24/1922CyyyyA²A	1926-1927	828	304a	66	

11.5. O24/1927C 4ᵗʰ 50% silver sixpence (1927-1946)

The last change in the base metal composition of the 50% silver coins took place at the moment that the coinage under George V was modernised in 1927. This zinc and nickel containing alloy continued to be in use until the removal of silver altogether from the general coinage in 1946.

Obverse A   *Obverse B*

Obverse A: Head of King George V facing left.

Obverse B: Head of King George VI facing left.

Reverse A   *Reverse B*

Reverse A: Six oak-sprigs with six acorns.

Reverse B: Crowned monogram. "IND IMP" in legend.

Type	Years	KM#	S#	Y#	X
O24/1927CyyyyAA	1927-1936	832	315	71	
O24/1927CyyyyBB	1937-1946	852	339	87	

11.6. O24/1947C Copper-nickel sixpence (1947-1970)

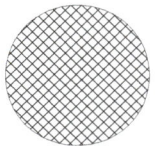

In 1947 silver was abolished from the British coins. After World War II the United Kingdom had accumulated so much debt that it was no longer possible to keep silver in the circulating currency and it was decided to replace it with copper-nickel. At first no changes were made to the designs of the coins and they could continue to circulate side by side. Of course when India became an independent country and later when Queen Elizabeth ascended to the throne changes were made. Although the last year on circulating sixpences is 1967 minting continued in later years due to demand until decimal day. Sixpences continued to be legal tender for 2½ new pence until 30 June 1980. This series has two obverse and three reverse designs.

Obverse A — *Obverse B¹* — *Obverse B²*

Obverse A: Head of King George VI facing left.

Obverse B¹: Head of Queen Elizabeth II facing right with "BRITT OMN" in legend.

Obverse B²: As obverse B¹ with "BRITT OMN" removed.

| *Reverse A* | *Reverse B* | *Reverse C* |

Reverse A: Crowned monogram "GRI"

Reverse B: Heavily redesigned crowned monogram "GviR". "IND IMP" removed.

Reverse C: Leek, rose thistle and shamrock interlaced.

Type	Years	KM#	S#	Y#	X
O24/1947CyyyyAA	1947-1948	862	339a	95	
O24/1947CyyyyAB	1949-1952	875	357	108	
O24/1947CyyyyB¹C	1953	889	371	120	
O24/1947CyyyyB²C	1954-1970	903	389	130	

12. O25/ Decimal 3 pence (GBP 0.03)

The only 3 (new) pence coin series issued is the continuation of the Maundy (old) silver threepence.

Series	Years	Comp.	Mass (g)	Size (mm)	THK (mm)
O25/1971C	1971-....	Silver (92.5% Ag, 7.5% Cu)	1.4138	16	0.7

12.1. O25/1971C Maundy 3 pence (1971-....)

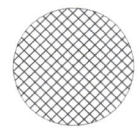

Continuation of the earlier Maundy threepence with no change in design or specification, but revalued from "old" to "new" pence.

Obverse: First head of Queen Elizabeth II facing right.

Reverse: Crowned "3" between divided date with wreath around.

Type	Years	KM#	S#	Y#	X
O25/1971Cyyyy	1971-...	901	397	C135	

13. O26/ Decimal 4 pence (GBP 0.05)

The only 4 (new) pence coin series issued is the continuation of the Maundy (old) silver fourpence.

Series	Years	Comp.	Mass (g)	Size (mm)	THK (mm)
O26/1971C	1971-....	Silver (92.5% Ag, 7.5% Cu)	1.8851	18	0.7

13.1. O26/1971C Maundy 4 pence (1971-....)

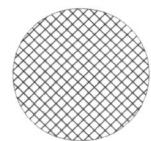

Continuation of the earlier Maundy fourpence with no change in design or specification, but revalued from "old" to "new" pence.

Obverse: First head of Queen Elizabeth II facing right.

Reverse: Crowned "4" between divided date with wreath around.

Type	Years	KM#	S#	Y#	X
O26/1971Cyyyy	1971-...	902	398	D135	

14. O27/ Shilling; 5 (new) pence (GBP 0.05)

The shilling ($^1/_{20}$ of a Pound) was originally just a money of account for the value of 12 (silver) pennies. Since about 1500 (King Henry VII) it is also minted as a coin. As a shilling is exactly equal to $^1/_{20}$ of a Pound, and thus after Decimal Day equal to 5 new pence shillings continued to be legal tender until the 5 pence coin was decreased in size in 1990, and was demonetised together with the older and larger 5 (new) pence coins that were actually produced with the same specifications as the last shilling coins. Due to the continuation from Shilling to 5 (new) pence a total of 8 coin series can be recognised. This includes 4 different 50% silver shilling series during the 1920s.

Series	Years	Comp.	Mass (g)	Size (mm)	THK (mm)
O27/1816C	1816-1919	Silver (92.5% Ag, 7.5% Cu)	5.67	24	1.2
O27/1920C	1920-1922	Silver (50% Ag, 40% Cu, 10% Ni)	5.67	24	1.2
O27/1921C	1921	Silver (50% Ag, 45% Cu, 5% Mn)	5.67	24	1.2
O27/1922C	1922-1927	Silver (50% Ag, 50% Cu)	5.67	24	1.2
O27/1927C	1927-1946	Silver (50% Ag, 40% Cu, 5% Zn, 5% Ni)	5.67	24	1.2
O27/1947C	1947-1990	Copper-nickel (75% Cu, 25% Ni)	5.67	24	1.4
O27/1990C	1990-2011	Copper-nickel (75% Cu, 25% Ni)	3.25	18	1.7
O27/2012C	2012-....	Nickel plated	3.25	18	1.7

Series	Years	Comp.	Mass (g)	Size (mm)	THK (mm)
		steel (94% steel with 6% Ni plating)			

14.1. O27/1816C Sterling silver shilling (1816-1919)

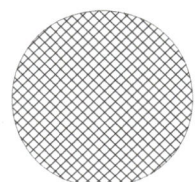

During the long lifetime of this series a total of 9 obverse and 8 reverse designs can be recognised. During the long reign of Queen Victoria several small variations in the designs are visible, although in many cases in higher quality specimens only.

Obverse A *Obverse B* *Obverse C*

Obverse D *Obverse E¹* *Obverse E²*

Obverse E³   *Obverse F¹*   *Oberse F²*

Obverse G   *Obverse H*   *Obverse I*

Obverse A: Head of King George III facing right.

Obverse B: Laureate head of King George IV facing left. Image from Bonneville (1849).

Obverse C: Bare head of King George IV facing left.

Obverse D: Head of King William IV facing right.

Obverse E¹: Young head of Queen Victoria facing left. Image from Bonneville (1849).

Obverse E²: As obverse E¹ but lower relief.

Obverse E³: As obverse E¹ but slightly aged.

Obverse F¹: Jubilee head of Queen Victoria facing left.

Obverse F²: Much larger Jubilee head of Queen Victoria.

Obverse G: Veiled head of Queen Victoria facing left.

Obverse H: Head of King Edward VI facing right.

Obverse I: Head of King George V facing left.

Reverse A

Reverse B

Reverse C

Reverse D

Reverse E¹

Reverse E²

Reverse E³

Reverse F¹

Reverse F²

Reverse G

Reverse H

Reverse A: Crowned shield within Garter.

Reverse B: Garnished shield with large crown. Image from Bonneville (1849).

Reverse C: Crowned shield within Garter. The shield is more or less square. Image from Bonneville (1849).

Reverse D: Lion on crown with rose, thistle and shamrock

below.

Reverse E^1: Crowned "ONE SHILLING" within wreath.

Reverse E^2: As reverse E^1 with die number above date.

Reverse E^3: As reverse E^1 but larger wording "ONE SHILLING".

Reverse F^1: Crowned shield within Garter. Different from reverse C in removal of Hanover shield, different crown and different age.

Reverse F^2: Slightly altered obverse F^1; Different drawing of crown (lines in stead of jewels) and no loop inside "Q" of the word "QUI" on Garter.

Reverse G: Three shields within Garter.

Reverse H: Lion on imperial crown within circle.

Type	Years	KM#	S#	Y#	X
O27/1816CyyyyAA	1816-1820	666	47		
O27/1816CyyyyBB	1821	679	59		
O27/1816CyyyyBC	1823-1825	687	63		
O27/1816CyyyyCD	1825-1829	694	66		
O27/1816CyyyyDE^1	1831-1837	713	84		
O27/1816CyyyyE^{1}E^1	1838-1863	734.1	101	6	
O27/1816CyyyyE^{1}E^2	1864-1867	734.3	102	6	
O27/1816CyyyyE^{2}E^2	1867-1879	734.2	102	6	
O27/1816CyyyyE^{3}E^1	1879	734.4	103	6	
O27/1816CyyyyE^{3}E^3	1880-1887	734.4	103	6	
O27/1816CyyyyF^{1}F^1	1887-1889	761	127	20	
O27/1816CyyyyF^{2}F^2	1889-1892	774	127	21	
O27/1816CyyyyGG	1893-1901	780	142	37	
O27/1816CyyyyHH	1902-1910	800	289	51	
O27/1816CyyyyIH	1911-1919	816	305	67	

14.2. O27/1920C 1ˢᵗ 50% silver shilling (1920-1922)

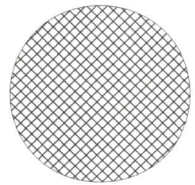

Due to rapidly increasing silver prices in 1920 it was decided to decrease the silver content in all silver coins from 92.5% to 50%. As the base metal part of the coins toned unattractive experiments were done with different base metal compositions until in 1927 a final composition was decided upon. The coins produced in each of these compositions are considered different coin series for the purpose of this catalogue, although there were no design changes. The first three 50% silver shillings all have (initially) the same design as O27/1816CyyyyIH.

Obverse   *Reverse*

Obverse: Head of King George V facing left.

Reverse: Lion on imperial crown within circle.

Type	Years	KM#	S#	Y#	X
O27/1920Cyyyy	1920-1922	816a	305a	67	

14.3. O24/1921C 2nd 50% silver shilling (1921)

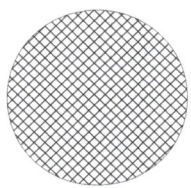

In 1921 experiments were also done with a 50% silver containing some manganese in stead of nickel. Apparently these experiments were not successful and the composition was revered back to the nickel containing silver. The shillings in this series are undistinguishable from the former, and they have the same design as O27/1816CyyyyIH.

Obverse   *Reverse*

Obverse: Head of King George V facing left.

Reverse: Lion on imperial crown within circle.

Type	Years	KM#	S#	Y#	X
O27/1921Cyyyy	1921	816a	305a	67	

14.4. O27/1922C 3ʳᵈ 50% silver shilling (1922-1927)

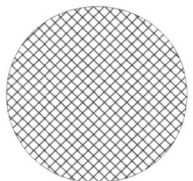

Initially the same design as O27/1816CyyyyIH. In 1926 the "modified" effigy of King George V started to be used. Due to size and wear the two obverses for the 1926 coins are very difficult to tell apart on lesser quality coins.

Obverse A¹   *Obverse A²*   *Reverse A*

Obverse A¹: Head of King George V facing left. The signature of the designer as "B.M." more or less in the middle of the truncation of the King's neck.

Obverse A²: Modified effigy of King George V, signature of designer as "BM" with no stops and more to the right of the truncation of the King's neck.

Reverse: Lion on imperial crown within circle.

Type	Years	KM#	S#	Y#	X
O27/1922CyyyyA¹A	1922-1926	816a	305a	67	
O27/1922CyyyyA²A	1926-1927	829	305a	67	

14.5. O27/1927C 4th 50% silver shilling (1927-1946)

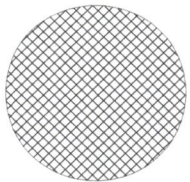

The last change in the base metal composition of the 50% silver coins took place at the moment that the coinage under George V was modernised in 1927. This zinc and nickel containing alloy continued to be in use until total removal of silver from circulating currency in the United Kingdom. During the reigns of King George VI and Queen Elizabeth II two versions of the shilling were issued, one with the English shield and one with the Scottish. Two obverse and two revere designs, although small differences between the "English" designs from both kings can be observed, especially in the placement of the date and the font type.

Obverse A   *Obverse B*

Obverse A: Head of King George V facing left.

Obverse B: Head of King George VI facing left.

Reverse A¹   *Reverse A²*   *Reverse B*

Reverse A[1]: Lion on imperial crown. The lion and crown are viewed from a different angle as compared the the earlier reverse from King George V shillings.

Reverse A[2]: Same lion as reverse A[1], but date divided with lion between and different font type in legend (English design).

Reverse B: Lion sitting on crown (Scottish design).

Type	Years	KM#	S#	Y#	X
O27/1927CyyyyAA[1]	1927-1936	833	316	72	
O27/1927CyyyyBA[2]	1937-1946	853	340	88	
O27/1927CyyyyBB	1937-1946	854	341	89	

14.6. O27/1947C Copper-nickel shilling and larger 5 (new) pence coins (1947-1990)

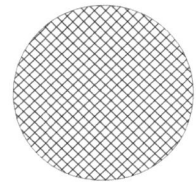

In 1947 silver was abolished from the British coins. After World War II the United Kingdom had accumulated so much debt that it was no longer possible to keep silver in the circulating currency and it was decided to replace it with copper-nickel. Although Decimal Day was in 1971, and this was the official moment that the United Kingdom decimalised the last year shillings were minted for circulation was in 1966 (although a few more were minted in 1967, but these also had 1966 as mintage year on them). In 1968 the first 5 new pence coins were issued. Until 1971 these coins were valid for 1 shilling and they were issued at this early date to facilitate a smooth changeover to the new system. The composition and size of the 5 new pence coins was exactly the same as the old shilling coins justifying both under this heading. Just like the older silver shillings they continued to be issued with both an English and a Scottish design until the end of the old system. 5 new pence coins were no longer issued with two designs. In total four obverse and five reverse designs were issued. Due to changes in the political situation of the British Empire both the coins of King George VI and Queen Elizabeth II observed changes in legends. The 5 (new) pence coin also was issued in two varieties due to the change from new pence to just pence in 1982.

Obverse A   Obverse B¹   Obverse B²

Obverse C   Obverse D

Obverse A: Head of King George VI facing left.

Obverse B¹: First head of Queen Elizabeth II facing right.

Obverse B²: As obverse B¹ but "BRITT OMN" removed.

Obverse C: Second head of Queen Elizabeth II facing right.

Obverse D: Third head of Queen Elizabeth II facing right.

Reverse A¹   Reverse A²   Reverse B¹

Reverse B²

Reverse C

Reverse D

Reverse E¹

Reverse E²

Reverse A¹: Lion on imperial crown (English design).

Reverse A²: As reverse A¹ but "IND IMP" removed.

Reverse B¹: Lion sitting on crown (Scottish design).

Reverse B²: As reverse B¹ but "IND IMP" removed.

Reverse C: Three leopards within crowned shield (English design).

Reverse D: Lion within crowned shield (Scottish design).

Reverse E¹: Crowned thistle between "NEW PENCE" and "5".

Reverse E²: As reverse E¹ but "FIVE PENCE".

Type	Years	KM#	S#	Y#	X
O27/1947CyyyyAA¹	1947-1948	863	340a	96	
O27/1947CyyyyAB¹	1947-1948	864	341a	97	
O27/1947CyyyyAA²	1949-1952	876	358	109	
O27/1947CyyyyAB²	1949-1951	877	359	110	
O27/1947CyyyyB¹C	1953	890	372	121	
O27/1947CyyyyB¹D	1953	891	373	122	
O27/1947CyyyyB²C	1954-1970	904	390	131	

Type	Years	KM#	S#	Y#	X
O27/1947CyyyyB²D	1954-1970	905	391	132	
O27/1947CyyyyCE¹	1968-1981	911	404		
O27/1947CyyyyCE²	1982-1984	929	419		
O27/1947CyyyyDE²	1985-1990	937	427		

14.7. O27/1990C Smaller copper-nickel 5 pence coin (1990-2011)

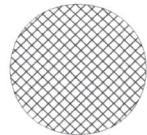

In 1990 a smaller version of the 5 pence coin was introduced to save on production costs of this coin but also because, due to inflation, the size of the coins was now considered too large in comparison to its purchasing power. Two obverse and two reverse designs are seen on these coins.

Obverse A *Obverse B¹* *Obverse B²*

Obverse A: Third head of Queen Elizabeth II facing right.

Obverse B¹: Fourth head of Queen Elizabeth II facing right. This obverse has a beaded border.

Obverse B²: As obverse B¹ with beading removed.

Reverse A   *Reverse B*

Reverse A: Crowned thistle between "FIVE PENCE" and "5".

Reverse B: Central part of shield of the royal arms.

Type	Years	KM#	S#	Y#	X
O27/1990CyyyyAA	1990-1997	937b	452		
O27/1990CyyyyB¹A	1998-2008	988	481		
O27/1990CyyyyB²B	2008-2011	1109	596		

14.8. O27/2012C Nickel plated steel 5 pence coin (2012-....)

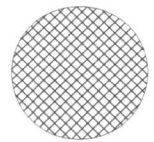

In 2012 the copper-nickel 5 pence coin was replaced by a nickel plated steel one in order to save (again) on production costs. In the first few years of its existence one reverse and two obverse designs were used.

Obverse A   *Obverse B*   *Reverse A*

Obverse A: Fourth head of Queen Elizabeth II facing right.

Obverse B: Fifth head of Queen Elizabeth II facing right.

Reverse A: Central part of shield of the royal arms.

Type	Years	KM#	S#	Y#	X
O27/2012CyyyyAA	2012-2015	1109d	596a		
O27/2012CyyyyBA	2015-....				

15. O30/ Florin (two shillings); 10 (new) pence (GBP 0.10)

Already in 1847 it was proposed that the United Kingdom would change its currency into a decimal one. The first step would be the introduction of a coin valued at two shillings or "one tenth of a Pound". This coin, the florin, was introduced in 1849 and the next year the slightly larger halfcrown (2 shillings and sixpence) was no longer minted. Apparently the halfcrown continued to be a popular coin and in 1874 minting and issuing was resumed. On the other hand, the florin was never abolished and as a result the strange situation arose that two coins with fairly similar values did circulated side by side for over 100 years in the United Kingdom.

Although the weight of the florin was clear from the beginning the diameter changed a few times during the 19th century. It started as a coin of 28 mm, increased to 30 mm in the second series, was reduced to 29.5 mm until it finally got its final size at 28.5 mm in 1893. As a result a fairly large number of series of florins/10 (new) pence can be recognised, four sterling silver series, four 50% silver series, two copper-nickel series and one nickel plated steel series. A total of eleven series thus. This includes of course the 10 (new) pence coins as at Decimal Day the florins could continue to circulate as 10 new pence coins with no change in specifications. Only when the copper-nickel coins were reduced in size in 1992 the old florin coins were removed from circulation.

Series	Years	Comp.	Mass (g)	Size (mm)	THK (mm)
O30/1849C	1849	Silver (92.5%	11.34	28	1.8

Series	Years	Comp.	Mass (g)	Size (mm)	THK (mm)
		Ag, 7.5% Cu)			
O30/1851C	1851-1887	Silver (92.5% Ag, 7.5% Cu)	11.34	30	1.5
O30/1887C	1887-1892	Silver (92.5% Ag, 7.5% Cu)	11.34	29.5	1.6
O30/1893C	1893-1919	Silver (92.5% Ag, 7.5% Cu)	11.34	28.5	1.7
O30/1920C	1920-1922	Silver (50% Ag, 40% Cu, 10% Ni)	11.34	28.5	1.8
O30/1921C	1921	Silver (50% Ag, 45% Cu, 5% Mn)	11.34	28.5	1.8
O30/1922C	1922-1926	Silver (50% Ag, 50% Cu)	11.34	28.5	1.8
O30/1927C	1927-1946	Silver (50% Ag, 40% Cu, 5% Zn, 5% Ni)	11.34	28.5	1.8
O30/1947C	1947-1992	Copper-nickel (75% CU, 25% Ni)	11.34	28.5	2.0
O30/1992C	1992-2011	Copper-nickel (75% Cu, 25% Ni)	6.5	24.5	1.85
O30/2012C	2012-....	Nickel plated steel (94% steel with 6% Ni plating)	6.5	24.5	1.85

15.1. O30/1849C 1ˢᵗ sterling silver florin (1849)

The florin didn't make a good start when the words "DEI GRATIA" were omitted from its first issue. For that reason it was minted for one year only (although a few may have been minted in 1950 and 1851) and it was replaced quickly with coins of a different type.

Obverse   *Reverse*

Obverse: Crowned "Gothic" head of Queen Victoria facing left.

Reverse: Four crowned cruciform shields with rose in centre. Legend, indicating a decimal coin "ONE FLORIN" "ONE TENTH OF A POUND".

Type	Years	KM#	S#	Y#	X
O30/1849Cyyyy	1849	745	104	7	

15.2. O30/1851C 2ⁿᵈ sterling silver florin (1851-1887)

The second florin was a lot more popular and lasted for 36 years. It was issued with effectively only one obverse and one reverse design. This design was the so called Gothic florin and was characterised by the fact that all legends were written in Gothic script and the date in Roman numerals. In spite of its long life only two (main) varieties of the obverse are recognised (and both with or without die numbers). It is to be realised however that several more minor varieties are known in this series. For a full understanding of these varieties more specialised literature, such as Rayner (1992) should be consulted.

Obverse A¹   *Obverse A³*   *Reverse A*

Obverse A¹: Crowned young ("Gothic") head of Queen Victoria facing left. Image from Homans & Mushet (1872).

Obverse A²: As obverse A² with die number below bust.

Obverse A³: As obverse A² (with die number) but portrait slightly aged.

Obverse A⁴: As obverse A³ without die number.

Reverse A: Four crowned cruciform shields with cross in centre. Legend as with O30/1849C1849 but written in

Gothic letters.

Type	Years	KM#	S#	Y#	X
O30/1851CyyyyA¹A	1851-1863	743.1	105	8	
O30/1851CyyyyA²A	1864-1867	743.3	106	8	
O30/1851CyyyyA³A	1868-1879	743.2	106	8	
O30/1851CyyyyA⁴A	1877-1887	743.4	107	8	

15.3. O30/1887C 3ʳᵈ sterling silver florin (1887-1892)

For the Jubilee issue of 1887 the florin was reduced in size by a half millimetre. The coin reverted to a more classic design. Only one obverse and reverse design.

Obverse　　　　　*Reverse*

Obverse: Jubilee head of Queen Victoria facing left.

Reverse: Cross made of the shields of England (twice), Scotland and Ireland with a star in the centre and sceptres between the shields.

Type	Years	KM#	S#	Y#	X
O30/1887Cyyyy	1887-1892	762	127	23	

15.4. O30/1893C 4ᵗʰ sterling silver florin (1893-1919)

Finally for the last issue of florins minted during the lifetime of Queen Victoria a lasting diameter for the florin was chosen. It is now 28.5 mm, a size it kept until the later 10 (new) pence coins were reduced in size in 1992. This 4ᵗʰ version of the sterling silver florin lasted until 1919 when the silver content of all British coins was reduced to 50%. During this period three obverse and three reverse designs were used.

Obverse A *Obverse C*

Obverse A: Veiled head of Queen Victoria facing left.

Obverse B: Head of King Edward VII facing right.

Obverse C: Head of King George V facing left.

Reverse A *Reverse C*

Reverse A: Three shields separated by rose, thistle and shamrock with Garter around.

Reverse B: Britannia standing holding shield and spear.

Reverse C: Cross made of shields with a star in the centre and sceptres between the shields.

Type	Years	KM#	S#	Y#	X
O30/1893CyyyyAA	1893-1901	781	143	38	
O30/1893CyyyyBB	1902-1910	801	290	52	
O30/1893CyyyyCC	1911-1919	817	306	68	

15.5. O30/1920C 1st 50% silver florin (1920-1922)

Due to rapidly increasing silver prices in 1920 it was decided to decrease the silver content in all silver coins from 92.5% to 50%. As the base metal part of the coins toned unattractive experiments were done with different base metal compositions until in 1927 a final composition was decided upon. The coins produced in each of these compositions are considered different coin series for the purpose of this catalogue, although there were no design changes. There was no design change when the silver content was decreased and in the 1st, 2nd and 3rd 50% silver series the design was the same as O30/1893CyyyyCC.

Obverse: Head of King George V facing left.

Reverse: Cross made of shields with a star in the centre and sceptres between the shields.

Type	Years	KM#	S#	Y#	X
O30/1920Cyyyy	1920-1922	817a	306a	68	

15.6. O24/1921C 2ⁿᵈ 50% silver florin (1921)

Also florins have been minted in 1921 and it is assumed that they also exist with the manganese containing alloy that was quickly abolished. These florins have the same design as O30/1893CyyyyCC.

     Obverse   *Reverse*

Obverse: Head of King George V facing left.

Reverse: Cross made of shields with a star in the centre and sceptres between the shields.

Type	Years	KM#	S#	Y#	X
O30/1921Cyyyy	1921	817a	306a	68	

15.7. O30/1922C 3ʳᵈ 50% silver florin (1922-1926)

The same design as O30/1893CyyyyCC. The florin is the

98

only silver coin that has not been minted with the "modified" effigy.

Obverse   *Reverse*

Obverse: Head of King George V facing left.

Reverse: Cross made of shields with a star in the centre and sceptres between the shields.

Type	Years	KM#	S#	Y#	X
O307/1922Cyyyy	1922-1926	817a	306a	68	

15.8. O30/1927C 4th 50% silver florin (1927-1946)

The last change in the base metal composition of the 50% silver coins took place at the moment that the coinage under George V was modernised in 1927. This zinc and nickel containing alloy continued to be in use until all silver was removed from the circulating currency in 1947. These coins are found in one version per reigning monarch.

Obverse A *Obverse B*

Obverse A: Head of King George V facing left.

Obverse B: Head of King George VI facing left.

Reverse A *Reverse B*

Reverse A: Cross made of shields with a star in the centre and sceptres between the shields. Completely redesigned from earlier King George V florins.

Reverse B: Crowned rose with thistle and shamrock left and right.

Type	Years	KM#	S#	Y#	X
O30/1927CyyyyAA	1927-1936	834	307	73	
O30/1927CyyyyBB	1937-1946	855	342	90	

15.9. O30/1947C Copper-nickel florin and larger 10 (new) pence coins (1947-1992)

In 1947 silver was abolished from the British coins and replace with copper-nickel. Although Decimal Day was in

1971, and this was the official moment that the United Kingdom decimalised the last year florins were minted for circulation was in 1967. The next year, in 1968 it was replaced by the 10 new pence coins which has the same physical and chemical characteristics. Until 1971 they were valid for 2 shillings (1 florin) and they were issued at this early date to facilitate a smooth changeover to the new system. In total four obverse and three reverse designs were issued. Due to changes in the political situation of the British Empire both the coins issued by King George VI and Queen Elizabeth II saw changes in legends. The 10 (new) pence coin also saw two varieties due to the change from new pence to just pence in 1982.

Obverse A   Obverse B¹   Obverse B²

Obverse C   Obverse D

Obverse A: Head of King George VI facing left.

Obverse B¹: First head of Queen Elizabeth II facing right.

Obverse B²: As obverse B¹ but "BRITT OMN" removed.

Obverse C: Second head of Queen Elizabeth II facing right.

Obverse D: Third head of Queen Elizabeth II facing right.

Reverse A¹

Reverse A²

Reverse B

Reverse C¹

Reverse C²

Reverse A¹: Crowned rose with thistle and shamrock left and right.

Reverse A²: As reverse A¹ but "IND IMP" removed.

Reverse B: Rose in the centre surrounded by thistle, shamrock and leeks.

Reverse C¹: Lion Passant between "NEW PENCE" and "10".

Reverse C²: As reverse E¹ but "TEN PENCE" above lion.

Type	Years	KM#	S#	Y#	X
O30/1947CyyyyAA¹	1947-1948	865	342a	98	
O30/1947CyyyyAA²	1949-1951	878	360	111	
O30/1947CyyyyB¹B	1953	892	374	123	
O30/1947CyyyyB²B	1954-1970	906	392	133	
O30/1947CyyyyCC¹	1968-1981	912	405		
O30/1947CyyyyCC²	1982-1984	930	420		
O30/1947CyyyyDC²	1985-1992	938	428		

15.10. O30/1992C Smaller copper-nickel 10 pence coin (1992-2011)

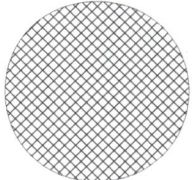

Two years after the reduction in size of the 5 pence coin also the size of the 10 pence coin was reduced for the same reasons. This series shows two obverse and two reverse designs.

Obverse A

Obverse B¹

Obverse B²

Obverse A: Third head of Queen Elizabeth II facing right.

Obverse B¹: Fourth head of Queen Elizabeth II facing right. This obverse has a beaded border.

Obverse B²: As obverse B¹ with beading removed.

Reverse A

Reverse B

Reverse A: Lion Passant between "TEN PENCE" and "10".

Reverse B: Upper left part of shield of the royal arms.

Type	Years	KM#	S#	Y#	X
O30/1992CyyyyAA	1992-1997	938b	454		

Type	Years	KM#	S#	Y#	X
O30/1992CyyyyB¹A	1998-2008	989	482		
O30/1992CyyyyB²B	2008-2011	1110	597		

15.11. O30/2012C Nickel plated steel 10 pence coin (2012-....)

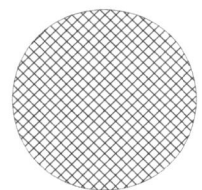

Just like the 5 pence coin in 2012 also the copper-nickel 10 pence coin was replaced by a nickel plated steel one in order to save (again) on production costs. In the first few years of its existence one reverse and two obverse designs were used.

Obverse A   *Obverse B*   *Reverse A*

Obverse A: Fourth head of Queen Elizabeth II facing right.

Obverse B: Fifth head of Queen Elizabeth II facing right.

Reverse A: Central part of shield of the royal arms.

Type	Years	KM#	S#	Y#	X
O30/2012CyyyyAA	2012-2015	1110d	597a		
O30/2012CyyyyBA	2015-....				

16. O31/ Halfcrown (GBP 0.12½)

The halfcrown, a coin with a value of 2 shillings and sixpence, or ⅛ of a Pound, was minted for the first time, as a gold coin, in 1526 under King Henry VIII. Since 1551 it is a silver coin, first minted under King Edward VI. After the Great Recoinage it was minted regularly except for a break of 25 years after the introduction of the florin. Apparently this coin continued to be very popular and as a result mintage was resumed in 1874. The halfcrown remained a popular coin right until the end of the predecimal era. It was demonetised on 1 January 1970, so that the halfcrowns issued in the farewell set of predecimal crowns from 1970 never were legal tender. Six series of halfcrowns were issued between 1816 and 1970, all with the same physical specifications. The silver content originally was $^{925}/_{1000}$, it was decreased to $^{500}/_{1000}$ in 1920 and was completely removed in favour of copper-nickel in 1947.

Series	Years	Comp.	Mass (g)	Size (mm)	THK (mm)
O31/1816C	1816-1919	Silver (92.5% Ag, 7.5% Cu)	14.175	32	1.7
O31/1920C	1920-1922	Silver (50% Ag, 40% Cu, 10% Ni)	14.175	32	1.7
O31/1921C	1921	Silver (50% Ag, 45% Cu, 5% Mn)	14.175	32	1.7
O31/1922C	1922-1927	Silver (50% Ag, 50% Cu)	14.175	32	1.7
O31/1927C	1927-1946	Silver (50% Ag, 40% Cu, 5% Zn, 5% Ni)	14.175	32	1.7
O31/1947C	1947-1990	Copper-nickel (75% Cu, 25% Ni)	14.175	32	2.0

16.1. O31/1816C Sterling silver halfcrown (1816-1919)

During the long lifetime of this series 10 obverse and 10 reverse designs have been used. During the long reign of Queen Victoria several minor variations in the designs are recognisable, although in many cases these are only visible in higher quality specimens. They are not mentioned in this catalogue and specialised literature should be consulted for a full understanding of these design variations (such as Davies, 1982 or Rayner, 1992. Also more general catalogues such as Lobel, 1996 or Perkins, 2014 will however be very useful to understand the existence of these minor variations).

Obverse A   Obverse B   Obverse C

Obverse D   Obverse E   Obverse F[1]

Obverse G

Obverse H

Obverse I

Obverse A: Large head of King George III facing right. Image from Bonneville (1849).

Obverse B: Smaller head of King George III facing right.

Obverse C: Laureate head of King George IV facing left. Image from Bonneville (1849).

Obverse D: Bare head of King George IV facing left. Image from Bonneville (1849).

Obverse E: Head of King William IV facing right. Image from Bonneville (1849).

Obverse F^1: Young head of Queen Victoria facing left. Image from Bonneville (1849).

Obverse F^2: As obverse E^1 but lower relief.

Obverse G: Jubilee head of Queen Victoria facing left.

Obverse H: Veiled head of Queen Victoria facing left.

Obverse I: Head of King Edward VI facing right.

Obverse J: Head of King George V facing left.

Reverse A

Reverse B

Reverse C

Reverse D

Reverse E

Reverse F

Reverse G

Reverse H

Reverse I

Reverse J[1]

Reverse A: Crowned shield within Garter. Image from Bonneville (1849).

Reverse B: Larger crowned shield within Garter.

Reverse C: Crowned shield with rose below, thistle to left and shamrock to right. Image from Bonneville (1849).

Reverse D: Crowned more of less square shield within Garter. Image from Bonneville (1849).

Reverse E: Shield with helmet and crown above. No Garter. Image from Bonneville (1849).

Reverse F: Crowned shield with mantle. Image from Bonneville (1849).

Reverse G: Crowned shield within branches with leaves. Image from Bonneville (1849).

Reverse H: Shield crowned with imperial crown with Garter and legend around.

Reverse I: Crowned "spade" formed shield.

Reverse J¹: Differently designed crowned shield within Garter and legend. Circle of beads between Garter and legend.

Reverse J²: As reverse J¹ without beaded circle.

Type	Years	KM#	S#	Y#	X
O31/1816CyyyyAA	1816-1817	667	48		
O31/1816CyyyyBB	1817-1820	672	48A		
O31/1816CyyyyCC	1820-1823	676	60		
O31/1816CyyyyCD	1823-1824	688	64		
O31/1816CyyyyDE	1824-1829	695	67		
O31/1816CyyyyEF	1831-1837	714	85		
O31/1816CyyyyF¹G	1839-1864	740	109	9	
O31/1816CyyyyF²G	1874-1887	756	109	9	
O31/1816CyyyyGH	1887-1892	764	129	24	
O31/1816CyyyyHI	1893-1901	782	144	39	
O31/1816CyyyyIJ¹	1902-1910	802	291	53	
O31/1816CyyyyJJ²	1911-1919	818.1	307	69	

16.2. O31/1920C 1ˢᵗ 50% silver halfcrown (1920-1922)

Due to rapidly increasing silver prices in 1920 it was decided to decrease the silver content in all silver coins from 92.5% to 50%. As the base metal part of the coins toned unattractive experiments were done with different base metal compositions until in 1927 a final composition was decided upon. The coins produced in each of these compositions are considered different coin series for the purpose of this catalogue, although there were no design changes. All coins have the same design as O31/1816CyyyyJJ[2].

Obverse: Head of King George V facing left.

Reverse: Crowned shield within Garter and legend. No beads between Garter and legend.

Type	Years	KM#	S#	Y#	X
O31/1920Cyyyy	1920-1922	818.1a	307a	69	

16.3. O24/1921C 2nd 50% silver halfcrown (1921)

Also halfcrowns have been minted in 1921 and it is assumed that they also exist with the manganese containing alloy that was quickly abolished. These halfcrowns have the same design as O31/1816CyyyyJJ[2].

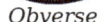
Obverse   *Reverse*

Obverse: Head of King George V facing left.

110

Reverse: Crowned shield within Garter and legend. No beads between Garter and legend.

Type	Years	KM#	S#	Y#	X
O31/1921Cyyyy	1921	818.1a	306a	68	

16.4. O31/1922C 3rd 50% silver halfcrown (1922-1926)

There is a small difference in the reverse design compared to the earlier issued of halfcrowns from King George V. On this reverse there is a larger distance ("a groove" between the crown and the shield. The obverse is minted from 1926 with the "modified effigy".

Obverse A¹   *Reverse A*

Obverse A¹: Head of King George V facing left. The signature of the designer as "B.M." more or less in the middle of the truncation of the King's neck.

Obverse A²: Modified effigy of King George V, signature of designer as "BM" with no stops to the right of the truncation of the King's neck.

Reverse: Crowned shield within Garter and legend. No beads between Garter and legend. Groove between the crown and the shield.

Type	Years	KM#	S#	Y#	X
O31/1922CyyyyA¹A	1922-1926	818.2	307	69	
O31/1922CyyyyA²A	1926-1927	830	307	69	

16.5. O31/1927C 4ᵗʰ 50% silver halfcrown (1927-1946)

The British silver coinage was modernised considerably in 1927, a change that appeared concurrently with the last change in composition of the 50% silver coins. Especially the reverse of the halfcrown got a design that was much more sharply than the design that were common since the Veiled head of Queen Victoria. Two obverse designs (one for each king) but only one reverse design that was slightly updated when King George VI ascended to the throne.

Obverse A   *Obverse B*

Obverse A: Head of King George V facing left

Obverse B: Head of King George VI facing left.

Reverse A¹   *Reverse A²*

Reverse A¹: Shield with monograms to left and right.

Reverse A²: As reverse A¹ but shield hanging from a nail and slightly different font type.

Type	Years	KM#	S#	Y#	X
O31/1927CyyyyAA¹	1927-1936	835	318	74	
O31/1927CyyyyBA²	1937-1946	856	343	91	

16.6. O31/1947C Copper-nickel halfcrown (1947-1970)

As with all silver coins the halfcrown was also issued as a copper-nickel coin from 1947. Its weight and size did not change and officially the older coins continued to be legal tender. The halfcrown was demonetised prior to Decimal Day on 1 January 1970, and as a result the 1970 halfcrown that was mined for the farewell proof set of 1970 never was legal tender. This last series of halfcrowns was issued with two obverse and two reverse designs, one for each monarch that served during the period this series was issued.

Obverse A   *Obverse B¹*   *Obverse B²*

Obverse A: Head of King George VI facing left.

Obverse B¹: First head of Queen Elizabeth II facing right.

Obverse B²: As obverse B¹ but "BRITT OMN" removed.

Reverse A¹   *Reverse A²*   *Reverse B*

Reverse A¹: Shield of the Royal Arms hanging from a nail.

Reverse A²: As reverse A¹ but "IND IMP" removed.

Reverse B: Crowned shield of the Royal Arms with monogram "E" and "R" to the left and right.

Type	Years	KM#	S#	Y#	X
O31/1947CyyyyAA¹	1947-1948	866	343a	99	
O31/1947CyyyyAA²	1949-1952	879	361	112	
O31/1947CyyyyB¹B	1953	893	375	124	
O31/1947CyyyyB²B	1954-1970	907	393	134	

17. O33/ Double florin; 20 pence (GBP 0.20)

The double florin (4 shillings) was issued for four years only as part of the Jubilee coinage of Queen Victoria. With a size of 36 mm it was only slightly smaller than a crown and in the dark it could possible be passed on for a crown. Officially this coin has never been demonetised and as a result it is currently still legal tender for 20 pence. The next coin with a face value of one fifth of a Pound was the 20 pence coin introduced in 1982 and from the onset one of the most popular and well used modern coins. This last coin series is minted as an equilateral curved heptagon.

Series	Years	Comp.	Mass (g)	Size (mm)	THK (mm)
O33/1887C	1887-1890	Silver (92.5% Ag, 7.5% Cu)	22.68	36	2.1
O33/1982C	1982-....	Copper-nickel (84% Cu, 16% Ni)	5	21.4	1.7

17.1. O33/1887C Double florin (1887-1890)

The double florin was issued as a second coin that would fit within a decimal system. Although regularly found in well worn form, indicating that it saw considerable circulation it never became a popular coin and was discontinued already after four years. As the coin was only slightly smaller than the more familiar crown, but 20% less valuable it was occasionally passed off for a crown. Especially barmaids, working in the fairly dark bars could be fooled with it and as they were liable for their own losses they then had to pay the landlord the loss. In a time that a shilling was a considerable sum of money this could cause large troubles and as such this coin was sometimes nicknamed "the barmaid's ruin". Only one obverse and one reverse design were used in this series.

Obverse   *Reverse*

Obverse: Jubilee head of Queen Victoria facing left.

Reverse: Four crowned shields in the form of a cross with sceptres between them. This design is much alike the reverse design of the Jubilee florin.

Type	Years	KM#	S#	Y#	X
O33/1887Cyyyy	1887-1890	763	130	25	

17.2. O33/1982C 20 pence (1982-....)

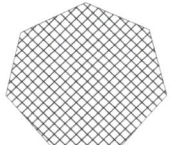

This coin is issued in the form of an equilateral curve heptagon. This form makes that it rolls properly when introduced into a vending machine, will for the eye it has a very characteristic form and makes it easy to distinguish from all other coins. This series was introduced in 1982 and remained a popular one with, since its inception, four different obverse and two different reverse designs.

Obverse A   *Obverse B*   *Obverse C[1]*

Obverse C²   *Obverse D*

Obverse A: Second head of Queen Elizabeth II facing right.

Obverse B: Third head of Queen Elizabeth II facing right.

Obverse C¹: Fourth head of Queen Elizabeth II facing right.

Obverse C²: As obverse C¹ with date moved to obverse.

Obverse D: Fifth head of Queen Elizabeth II facing right.

Reverse A   *Reverse B*

Reverse A: Crowned double rose.

Reverse B: Centre right part of the shield of the Royal Arms.

Type	Years	KM#	S#	Y#	X
O33/1982CyyyyAA	1982-1984	931	421		
O33/1982CyyyyBA	1985-1997	939	429		
O33/1982CyyyyC¹A	1998-2008	990	483		
O33/1982CyyyyC²B	2008-2015	1111	598		
O33/1982CyyyyDB	2015-....				

18. O34/ Crown (GBP 0.25)

Perhaps the most famous of the silver coins. Due to its size it is possible to put many details in the designs and these coins were often the magnificent centrepieces of the 19th century proof sets that were regularly issued to commemorate a new monarch or a new coinage design. In spite of its fame the mintage figures of all crowns are very modest. Although issued crowns often showed considerable circulation, as in many cases well worn specimens are found its purchasing value was so high that it was not a convenient coin for daily commerce. As a silver coin it was only legal tender for up to 40 shillings, so that never more than eight crowns could be offered for payment of goods, and gold coins such as the half sovereign and the sovereign which were legal tenter to any amount were much more convenient coins for larger payments. As a result not only the mintages of the individual crowns were relatively low, they were also issued quite irregularly. During the long reign of Queen Victoria for example only four issues are known, one of which was as proof coins only. During the 20th century the crowns finally developed into commemorative coins only, and all issues after the inauguration coin of King George VI are treated as commemorative coins and no attempts have been made to describe these coins in detail or to show images of these coins. After Decimal Day commemorative crowns continued to be issued as 25 new pence coins, the last of which was issued in 1981. They were never demonetised and are formally still legal tender for 25 pence. Three series of crowns have been issued since 1816, a sterling silver, a 50% silver and a copper-nickel.

Series	Years	Comp.	Mass (g)	Size (mm)	THK (mm)
O34/1818C	1818-1902	Silver (92.5% Ag, 7.5% Cu)	28.35	38.61	2.3
O34/1927C	1927-1937	Silver (50% Ag, 40% Cu, 5% Zn, 5% Ni)	28.35	38.61	2.4
O34/1951C	1951-1981	Copper-nickel (75% Cu, 25% Ni)	28.28	38.61	2.89

18.1. O34/1818C Sterling silver crown (1818-1902)

Crowns were issued irregularly. They were issued as circulation coins on a regular bases between 1818 and 1826 during the reigns of the Kings George III and George IV, and between 1844 and 1847 and between 1887 and 1902 during the reigns of Queen Victoria and King Edwards VII only. It is some kind of a surprise that no crown was issued when King George V was crowned. A total of nine obverse and six reverse designs have been used on these coins.

| Obverse A | Obverse B | Obverse C |
| Obverse D | Obverse E | Obverse F |

119

Obverse G

Obverse A: Head of King George III facing right. Image from de Bonneville (1849).

Obverse B: Laureate head of King George IV facing left. Image from de Bonneville (1849).

Obverse C: Bare head of King George IV facing left. Image from de Bonneville (1849).

Obverse D: Head of King William IV facing right. Image from de Bonneville (1849).

Obverse E: Young head of Queen Victoria facing left. Image from de Bonneville (1849).

Obverse F: Crowned young head of Queen Victoria facing left. This is the so called "Gothic" type obverse, comparable to the "Gothic" florin. Image from Homans & Mushet (1872).

Obverse G: Jubilee head of Queen Victoria facing left.

Obverse H: Veiled head of Queen Victoria facing left.

Obverse I: Head of King Edward VII facing right.

Reverse A

Reverse B¹

Reverse B²

Reverse C

Reverse D

Reverse E

Reverse F

Reverse A: St George slaying the dragon with Garter around. Image from de Bonneville (1849).

Reverse B[1]: St George slaying the dragon. Helmet of St George has no streamer. Image from de Bonneville (1849).

Reverse B[2]: As reverse B[1], but helmet has a streamer.

Reverse C: Crowned garnished shield showing wonderful details. Image from de Bonneville (1849).

Reverse D: Crowned shield on mantle. Image from de Bonneville (1849).

Reverse E: Crowned shield with branches around. Image from de Bonneville (1849).

Reverse F: "Gothic" type, cross with shields and Gothic lettering in legend with mintage year in Roman numerals. Image from Homans & Mushet (1872).

Type	Years	KM#	S#	Y#	X
O34/1818CyyyyAA	1818-1820	675	49		
O34/1818CyyyyBB[1]	1821-1823	680	61		
O34/1818CyyyyCC	1825-1826	699	67A		
O34/1818CyyyyDD	1831	715	85A		
O34/1818CyyyyEE	1839-1847	741	109	10	

Type	Years	KM#	S#	Y#	X
O34/1818CyyyyFF	1847-1853	744	108	11	
O34/1818CyyyyGB²	1887-1892	765	131	26	
O34/1818CyyyyHB²	1893-1900	783	145	40	
O34/1818CyyyyIB²	1902	803	292	54	

Types O34/1818CyyyyDD and O34/1818CyyyyEE were only issued in very small numbers as proof coins.

18.2. O34/1927C 50% silver crown (1927-1937)

The first crown issued by King George V was the well known Wreath crown in the proof set from 1927. As the coins appeared to be popular it was decided to issued this type every year, but only on order. In all years until the end of the reign of the King small numbers, up to several thousands were ordered and minted each year, mostly to be given as keepsakes for Christmas. The 1935 issue celebrating the King's Silver Jubilee is the first real commemorative coin issued in the United Kingdom. Although the 1937 crown can be considered, and probably is actually a commemorative crown its design is classic and for that reason for this catalogue considered a regular circulating coin, the last in the crown series.

Obverse A: Head of King George V facing left.

Obverse B: Head of King George VI facing left.

Reverse A: Imperial crown within wreath.

Reverse B: Crowned Royal Arms supported by lion and unicorn.

Type	Years	KM#	S#	Y#	X
O34/1927CyyyyAA	1927-1936	836	319	75	
O34/1927CyyyyBB	1937	857	344	92	
O34?1927CyyyyZ	1935	Commemorative design			

18.3. O34/1951C Copper-nickel crown (1951-1981)

Issued as eight (8) commemorative issues only, four of these predecimal as 5 shillings coins and four decimal as 25 new pence coins.

19. O37/ 10 shillings; 50 (new) pence (GBP 0.50)

The 10 shilling denomination reflects a break in the listings of United Kingdom coins and paper money. All listings up to this point consisted of silver and bronze coins. The 10 shillings is both the smallest gold coin that was issued in the United Kingdom, as well as the lowest paper money denomination that was in real use. Paper money with values less than 10 shillings has been prepared for circulation in the past, both by the treasury and by the Bank of England, but these were never issued to the general public. For that reason it is omitted from this catalogue. Gold coins were issued as circulating money until the outbreak of World War I. It was then quickly replaced by treasury notes. After Word War I gold coins were never circulating again in the United Kingdom and they were permanently replaced by Treasury notes until 1927 and Bank of England notes after that year. Due to inflation the value of 10 shilling decreased to such an extend that, with decimalisation in sight, in 1969 the 10 shilling banknote was replaced with a 50 new pence coin. After reduction in size in 1997 the 50 pence coin is still in circulation and it is the lowest value coin that is used for commemorative issues. Gold 10 shilling coins, the so called half sovereigns, were, except for a few issues to provide continuity in the series, were again being issued regularly from 1980. These modern coins are issued mostly as bullion coins, traded at their gold value, or proof coins issued for collectors. Although they are no longer issued and traded at face value the continuity of the series justifies incorporation of half sovereigns in this catalogue (just like the Maundy coins). In recent years several commemorative designs have been issued, these however are not described in here, only the regular designs that are issued on the bullion coins are described.

In total 9 series of 10 shilling/50 pence coins and notes can be recognised. They are split in two gold coin series, five note series (three Treasury and two Bank of England series) and two copper-nickel coin series.

Series	Years	Comp.	Mass (g)	Size (mm)	THK (mm)
O37/1817C	1817-....	Gold (91.7% Au, 8.3% Cu)	3.99	19.3	0.8
O37/1831C	1831-1834	Gold (91.7% Au, 8.3% Cu)	3.99	17.9	0.9
O37/1914N	1914	Paper		64x127	
O37/1915N	1915	Paper		76x136	
O37/1918C	1918	Paper		78x138	
O37/1928N	1928	Paper		78x138	
O37/1961N	1961	Paper		67x140	

Series	Years	Comp.	Mass (g)	Size (mm)	THK (mm)
O37/1969C	1969-1997	Copper-nickel (75% Cu, 25% Ni)	13.5	30	2.1
O37/1997C	1997-....	Copper-nickel (75% Cu, 25% Ni)	8	27.3	1.5

19.1. O37/1817C Large gold half sovereign (1817-....)

Issued with the current dimensions since 1817. Only between 1831 and 1834 experiments with a smaller sized coin were done, but after that last date it was reverted to the larger coin. The gold standard was finally abandoned in the United Kingdom in 1931. As the Pound was devalued also that year the value of the gold coins was now more than their legal value, and as such they could no longer be used for commercial payments at face value. The United Kingdom gold coins continued to be popular in certain areas such as the Middle East and they continued to circulate in these regions against their bullion values. Demand was such that in 1982 bullion half sovereigns were issued again. Proof versions were already issued from 1980 and are regularly issued each year since. In this catalogue only those half sovereigns of this series are described that follow the permanent designs, of which 20 obverse and 8 reverse designs can be recognised. Half sovereigns that were minted in the so called "branch" mints in Australia, Canada, India and South Africa are not classified here but will be classified in the catalogues of the countries where they were minted (and issued for the largest part).

Obverse A

Obverse B

Obverse D¹

Obverse E

Obverse H

Obverse I

Obverse L

Obverse N

Obverse A: Head of King George III facing right. Image from de Bonneville (1849).

Obverse B: Laureate head of King George IV facing left. Image from de Bonneville (1849).

Obverse C: Bare head of King George IV facing left.

Obverse D¹: Small head of King William IV facing right. This head is small because it was originally in use as obverse for the smaller coin O37/1831C. Image from de Bonneville (1849).

Obverse D²: Larger head of King William IV. This obverse is from the sixpence.

Obverse E: Young head of Queen Victoria facing left. Image from de Bonneville (1849).

Obverse F: Jubilee head of Queen Victoria facing left.

Obverse G: Veiled head of Queen Victoria facing left.

Obverse H: Head of King Edward VII facing right.

Obverse I: Head of King George V facing left.

Obverse J: Head of King George VI facing left.

Obverse K: First head of Queen Elizabeth II facing right.

Obverse L: Second head of Queen Elizabeth II facing right.

Obverse M: Third head of Queen Elizabeth II facing right.

Obverse N: Forth head of Queen Elizabeth II facing right.

Obverse O: Fifth head of Queen Elizabeth II facing right.

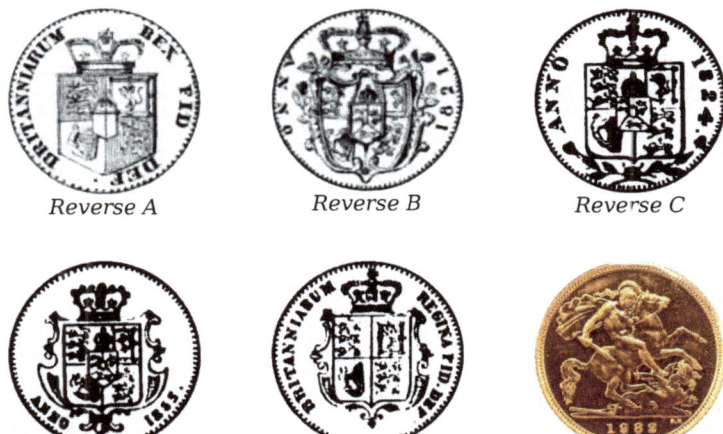

Reverse A   *Reverse B*   *Reverse C*

Reverse E   *Reverse F¹*   *Reverse H*

Reverse A: Crowned shield of the Royal Arms. Image from de Bonneville (1849).

Reverse B: Crowned shield garnished with rose, shamrock and thistle. Image from de Bonneville (1849).

Reverse C: Square crowned shield with garnish at foot only. Image from de Bonneville (1849).

Reverse D: Different shield, lightly garnished.

Reverse E: Different crowned shield with date below. No

legend. Image from de Bonneville (1849).

Reverse F[1]: Another different crowned and garnished shield. Image from de Bonneville (1849).

Reverse F[2]: As reverse F[1] with die number below shield.

Reverse G: Garnished shield with Imperial crown.

Reverse H: St. George slaying the dragon.

Type	Years	KM#	S#	Y#	X
O37/1817CyyyyAA	1817-1820	673	50		
O37/1817CyyyyBB	1821	681	68		
O37/1817CyyyyBC	1823-1825	689	69		
O37/1817CyyyyCD	1826-1828	700	71		
O37/1817CyyyyD^{1}E	1835-1837	722	86		
O37/1817CyyyyD^{2}E	1836-1837	722	86		
O37/1817CyyyyEF^1	1838-1886	735.1	111	13	
O37/1817CyyyyEF^2	1863-1877	735.2	112	13	
O37/1817CyyyyFG	1887-1893	766	132	28	
O37/1817CyyyyGH	1893-1901	784	146	42	
O37/1817CyyyyHH	1902-1910	804	293	56	
O37/1817CyyyyIH	1911-1915	819	308	77	
O37/1817CyyyyJH	1937	858	345	100	
O37/1817CyyyyKH	1953	Pn135	377		
O37/1817CyyyyLH	1980-1984	922	407		
O37/1817CyyyyMH	1985-1997	942	432		
O37/1817CyyyyNH	1998-2015	1001	491		
O37/1817CyyyyOH	2015-....				
O37/1817CyyyyZ	1989, 2002, 2005, 2016	Commemorative designs			

19.2. O37/1831C Small gold half sovereign (1831-1834)

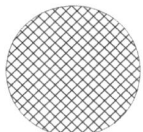

During the rein of King William IV tests were done with a smaller half sovereign apparently to be able to use the same tools as for the Maundy fourpence (Lobel, 1996). However, after one proof and one currency issue the coin was reverted back to the original size. Due to its short run only one obverse and one reverse design were used.

Obverse: Head of King William IV facing right.

Reverse: Crowned shield with date below. No legend.

Type	Years	KM#	S#	Y#	X
O37/1831Cyyyy	1831-1834	716, 720	86		

19.3. O37/1914N 1ˢᵗ series Treasury 10 shillings note

At the start of World War I it was clear that it was essential to keep as much gold as possible within the country. For that reason the government wanted to issue paper money as legal tender that was backed by the gold coins (that were then held in the government vaults) in stead of circulating the gold coins themselves. As the Bank of England was unable to issue paper money of new, low denominations in short notice the Treasury decided to issue them and paper money with denominations of 10 shillings and 1 Pound were issued within one week. It was able to do this job that fast by using postage stamp paper! The 1ˢᵗ issue was already issued in August 1914, printed on one side only, and signed by the Secretary to the Treasury John Bradbury.

Obverse

Obverse: Vignette of King George V to the left, large "Ten Shillings" in Gothic script along the note. The note is printed in red. The note is not dated, the issue date is taken from the Withdrawn Banknotes Reference Guide, issued by the Bank of England. As with all paper money images in this catalogue the image was taken from the Withdrawn Reference Guide published by the Bank of England on their website.

Reverse: Not printed.

Type	Issued	P#	X
O37/1914N	14 August 1914	346	

19.4. O37/1915N 2nd series Treasury 10 shillings note

Issued a few months after the former on better quality (banknote) paper.

Obverse

Obverse: Vignette of King George V in upper left corner, St. George slaying the dragon in the upper right corner. "TEN SHILLINGS" in centre of the note. Printed in red, not dated.

Reverse: Not printed.

Type	Issued	P#	X
O37/1915N	21 January 1915	348	

19.5. O37/1918N 3rd series Treasury 10 shillings note

A third series of 10 shilling Treasury notes was issued in 1918. This series lasted longer than the earlier and only stopped being issued after the Bank of England gained the responsibility of issuing banknotes of all values in England.

Obverse A¹

Obverse A¹: Vignette of King George V to the right. Standing Britannia to the left. "TEN SHILLINGS" in centre of note. Issued for "UNITED KINGDOM OF GREAT BRITAIN AND IRELAND". Printed in green.

Obverse A²: As obverse A¹ but issued for "UNITED KINGDOM OF GREAT BRITAIN AND NORTHERN IRELAND".

Reverse A: In green, "10 SHILLINGS" in centre.

Type	Issued/Signatures	P#	X
O37/1918NyyyyA¹A	22 October 1918; Bradbury (1918), Warren-Fisher (1919)	350, 356, 358	
O37/1818NyyyyA²A	Warren-Fisher (1927)	360	

Individual notes are catalogued as follows: O37/1918N1918A¹A for Bradbury notes and O37/1819N1919A¹A for Warren-Fisher notes. Black and red serial numbers can be distinguished after this code by "b" or "r".

19.6. O37/1928N Series A 10 shillings banknote

In 1928 the Bank of England took the responsibility to

issue also lower denomination (that is lower than 5 Pounds) banknotes. It is issued in two colour variations, and with or without security thread (in cataloguing this is considered to be part of the obverse).

Obverse A¹

Obverse A²

Obverse A³

Obverse A¹: Vignette of Britannia to the left and "10 SHILLINGS" to the right. Issuer and value in the centre of the note. Signature of Chief Cashier in lower left. This note is red-brown. No metal thread.

Obverse A²: As obverse A¹ but colour mauve and grey. Issued as a wartime emergency issue. Note includes metal thread.

Obverse A³: As obverse A¹ (colour red-brown) with metal tread included.

Reverse A¹

Reverse A²

Reverse A¹: Ornamental design including value of note as "10/-". The colour is red-brown.

Reverse A²: As reverse A¹, but colour is mauve and grey.

Type	Issued/Signatures	P#	X
O37/1928NyyyyA¹A¹	22 November 1928; Mahon (1928), Catterns (1929), Peppiatt (1934)*	362	
O37/1928NyyyyA²A²	2 April 1940; Peppiatt (1940)	366	
O37/1928NyyyyA³A¹	25 October 1948; Peppiatt (1948), Beale (1949), O'Brien (1955)	368	

*The first type was reissued for about four months in 1948 in order to use up pre-war banknote paper.

19.7. O37/1961N Series C 10 shillings banknote

Issued with one design only. The first (and only) 10 shillings banknote featuring a portrait of Queen Elizabeth II. This note was demonetised 13 October 1969 after it was replaced by the 50 new pence coin.

Obverse   *Reverse*

Obverse: Portrait of Queen Elizabeth II to the right, "Ten Shillings" in centre of note. The colour is red-brown.

Reverse: Sitting Britannia in centre, "TEN Shillings" below.

Type	Issued/Signatures	P#	X
O37/1961Nyyyy	12 October 1961; O'Brien (1961), Hollom (1962), Fforde (1966)	373	

19.8. O37/1969C Large 50 (new) pence coin (1969-1997)

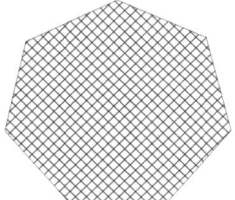

Issued in 1969 to replace the 10 shilling banknote in preparation for Decimal Day. It was the first equilaterial curved heptagonal coin in the world. Although this coin has a very distinctive heptagonal form a vending machine "sees" the coin as round so that it smoothly rolls through. This coin is the lowest value coin that was regularly used for circulating commemorative coins. Apart from these, two permanent obverse and one permanent reverse designs have been used on this coin.

Obverse A   *Obverse B*

Obverse A: Second head of Queen Elizabeth II facing right.

Obverse B: Third head of Queen Elizabeth II facing right.

Reverse A¹   *Reverse A²*

Reverse A¹: Seating Britannia between "NEW PENCE" and "50".

Reverse A²: As reverse A¹ but legend is "FIFTY PENCE".

Type	Years	KM#	S#	Y#	X
O37/1969CyyyyAA¹	1969-1981	913	406		
O37/1969CyyyyAA²	1982-1984	932	422		
O37/1969CyyyyBA²	1985-1997	940.1	430		
O37/1969CyyyyZ	1973, 1992, 1994	Commemorative designs			

19.9. O37/1997C Small 50 pence coin (1997-....)

In 1997 the size of the 50 pence coin was reduced as it was by then considered too large in relationship to its purchasing power. This coin is used almost every year since then as the denomination for commemorative coins. The number of commemorating coins could be as high as 30 as were issued during 2011 in anticipation of the 2012 London Olympic Games. The number of permanent designs is much lower, with three obverse and two reverse designs.

Obverse A

Obverse B¹

Obverse B²

Obverse C

Obverse A: Third head of Queen Elizabeth II facing right.

Obverse B¹: Fourth head of Queen Elizabeth II facing right. This obverse has a corner of the heptagon pointing up.

Obverse B²: As obverse B¹. This obverse has a corner of the heptagon pointing down.

Obverse C: Fifth head of Queen Elizabeth II facing right.

| *Reverse A* | *Reverse B* |

Reverse A: Seated Britannia.

Reverse B: Lower central part of the shield of the Royal Arms.

Type	Years	KM#	S#	Y#	X
O37/1997CyyyyAA	1997	940.2	467		
O37/1997CyyyyB¹A	1998-2008	991	484		
O37/1997CyyyyB²B	2008-2015	1112	599		
O37/1997CyyyyCB	2015-....				
O37/1997CyyyyZ	Almost all years		Commemorative designs		

20. O40/ 1 Pound (GBP 1.00)

The gold Pound coin was introduced with the Great Recoinage in 1816. It replaced the older Guinea, a gold coin valued at 21 shillings, but also the Bank of England one Pound banknotes. These banknotes continued to be in circulation for a while until most economic problems were solved in 1825/1826. As described above the gold coins (including the Pound coins or sovereigns) were largely replaced by paper money (Treasury notes) in 1914. Although currency gold coins were minted for a few more years they never became important in circulation anymore. Many, or even most of these last minted Pound coins (sovereigns) were sent to the United States as payment for war debts and melted after arrival. Most of the 20th century the Pound circulated as note, but inflation decreased the value of a Pound to such extend that in 1983 it was replaced again by a, now nickel-brass, coin. As this coin is counterfeited extensively the United Kingdom will introduce a new, 12 sided Pound coin, in 2017. Including the one Pound "white" banknotes from the early 19th century until now nine series of 1 Pounds have circulated since 1816. Two of these reflect coin series, the others either Treasury notes or Bank of England notes. The series below already incorporate the new Pound coin that will be introduced in 2017 for completion.

Series	Years	Comp.	Mass (g)	Size (mm)	THK (mm)
O40/1797N	1797-1826	Paper		appr. 113x200	
O40/1817C	1817-....	Gold (91.7% Au, 8.3% Cu)	7.98	22.05	1.2
O40/1914N¹	1914	Paper		64x127	
O40/1914N²	1914	Paper		83x149	
O40/1917N	1917	Paper		84x151	
O40/1928N	1928	Paper		85x151	
O40/1960N	1960	Paper		72x151	
O40/1978N	1978	Paper		67x135	
O40/1983C	1983-2016	Nickle-	9.5	22.5	3.15

Series	Years	Comp.	Mass (g)	Size (mm)	THK (mm)
		brass (70% Cu, 24.5% Zn, 5.5% Ni)			
O40/2017C	2017-....	Bimetellic*	8.61	22.7 (sides), 23.5 (corners)	2.8

*This coin will be 12-sided like the nickel-brass threepence coin (O21/1937C), but bimetallic with an outer ring made of nickel-brass and an inner disc that is made of a nickel plated non ferrous metal (such as copper-nickel?).

20.1. O40/1797N White 1 Pound banknote (1797-1826)

These uniface banknotes had a simple design indicating that the Bank would pay the bearer on demand the sum of 1 Pound. These notes were first issued in 1797 due to shortages in the gold supply. When enough gold Pound coins, sovereigns were minted after the Great Recoinage of 1816 these notes could be withdrawn again. These and other "white" notes, even when issued first before 1816 will only be cross-referenced with "P" numbers from the notes that were put in circulation in or after 1816, although older notes may be used as image as the images are taken form the Bank of England publication "Withdrawn Banknotes Reference Guide". Unlike the more recent banknotes issued since the 20th century white notes were dated.

Obverse

Type	Issued/Signatures	P#	X
O40/1797N	2 March 1797; Hase (1807)	130	

20.2. O40/1817C Gold sovereign (1817-....)

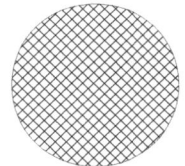

The gold sovereign (1 Pound coin) was first issued in 1817 and following years often in large quantities. They were a popular type of coins and circulated more or less world wide, which is not a surprise considering the size of the British Empire during the 19th and early 20th century. During World War I the gold coins were replaced by paper money and the last gold sovereign actually worth 1 Pound in gold was the 1925 issue. All sovereigns issued with dates beyond 1925 actually contained more than 1 Pound in gold when they were minted or issued. After the 1925 issue bullion sovereigns were minted again between 1957 and 1982 and since 2000. However, since 1980 proof versions have been minted every year. Although mostly traded for their gold content the series is incorporated here to indicate the continuity of this coin series. As the series almost runs for 200 years now a large amount (20!) obverse designs appear on these coins. The number of reverse designs is much smaller as since 1871 only the Saint George slaying the dragon reverse has been used on sovereigns. Before 1871 mostly the shield of the Royal Arms was used, and the total permanent reverse designs can be counted to 5. In recent years also a few commemorative obverse and reverse designs have used, but as with all commemoratives these are not detailed. Sovereigns that were minted in the so called "branch" mints in the colonies Australia, Canada, India and South Africa are not classified here but will be classified in the catalogues of the countries where they were minted (and issued for the largest part).

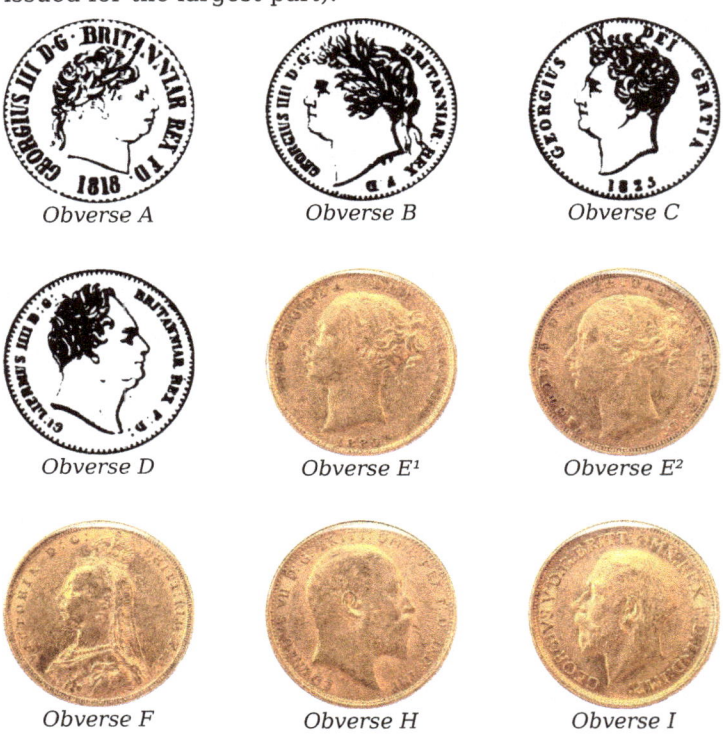

Obverse A *Obverse B* *Obverse C*

Obverse D *Obverse E¹* *Obverse E²*

Obverse F *Obverse H* *Obverse I*

Obverse N

Obverse A: Head of King George III facing right. Image from de Bonneville (1849).

Obverse B: Laureate head of King George IV facing left. Image from de Bonneville (1849).

Obverse C: Bare head of King George IV facing left. Image from de Bonneville (1849).

Obverse D: Head of King William IV facing right. Image from de Bonneville (1849).

Obverse E^1: Young head of Queen Victoria facing left. Date below head. Image is from a Sydney mint coin, so that the date on the image is beyond that for London coins as Sydney continued to strike shield sovereigns until a later date than London. Except for this there are no differences between London and Sydney coins.

Obverse E^2: As obverse E^1 but no date.

Obverse F: Jubilee head of Queen Victoria facing left.

Obverse G: Veiled head of Queen Victoria facing left.

Obverse H: Head of King Edward VII facing right.

Obverse I: Head of King George V facing left.

Obverse J: Head of King George VI facing left.

Obverse K^1: First head of Queen Elizabeth II facing right.

Obverse K^2: As obverse K^1 but "BRITT OMN" removed.

Obverse L: Second head of Queen Elizabeth II facing right.

Obverse M: Third head of Queen Elizabeth II facing right.,

Obverse N: Fourth head of Queen Elizabeth II facing right.

Obverse O: Fifth head of Queen Elizabeth II facing right.

Reverse A

Reverse B¹

Reverse B²

Reverse C

Reverse D

Reverse E¹

Reverse A: St. George slaying the dragon with Garter around. Image from de Bonneville (1849).

Reverse B¹: St George slaying the dragon. Date below and Garter removed. The streamer is missing from the helmet.

Reverse B²: As reverse B¹ but with streamer on helmet.

Reverse C: Crowned shield of the Royal Arms. Image from de Bonneville (1849).

Reverse D: Crowned shield, no legend around. Image from de Bonneville (1849).

Reverse E¹: Crowned shield with wreath around. Image is from a Sydney mint coin, indicated by the "S" mintmark. Except from this there is no difference from a London coin.

Reverse E²: As reverse E¹ with die number below Arms.

Type	Years	KM#	S#	Y#	X
O40/1817CyyyyAA	1817-1820	674	51		
O40/1817CyyyyAB¹	1821-1825	682	70		
O40/1817CyyyyCC	1825-1830	696	72		
O40/1817CyyyyDD	1831-1837	717	87		
O40/1817CyyyyE¹E¹	1838-1872	736.1	113	14	

Type	Years	KM#	S#	Y#	X
O40/1817CyyyyE¹E²	1863-1874	736.2	114	14	
O40/1817CyyyyE²B¹	1871-1885	752	115	15	
O40/1817CyyyyFB²	1887-1892	767	133	29	
O40/1817CyyyyGB²	1893-1901	785	147	43	
O40/1817CyyyyHB²	1902-1910	805	294	57	
O40/1817CyyyyIB²	1911-1925	820	309	78	
O40/1817CyyyyJB²	1937	859	346	101	
O40/1817CyyyyK¹B²	1953	Pn136	378		
O40/1817CyyyyK²B²	1957-1968	908	394	137	
O40/1817CyyyyLB²	1974-1984	919	408		
O40/1817CyyyyMB²	1985-1997	943	433		
O40/1817CyyyyNB²	1998-2008	1002	492		
O40/1817CyyyyNB¹	2009-2015	1252	492		
O40/1817CyyyyOB¹	2015-....				
O40/1817CyyyyZ	e.g. 1989, 2002, 2005, 2012, 2016		Commemorative designs		

20.3. O40/1914N¹ 1ˢᵗ series Treasury 1 Pound note

At the start of World War I also 1 Pound notes needed to be issued as quickly as possible. Just like the 10 shillings note the Treasury managed to issue these notes within one week's time. It was able to do this job that fast by using postage stamp paper. This 1ˢᵗ issue was issued in August 1914, printed on one side only, and signed by the Secretary to the Treasury John Bradbury.

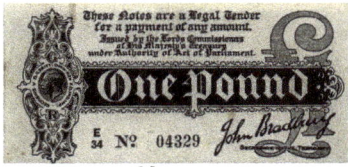
Obverse

Obverse: Vignette of King George V to the left, large "One

Pound" in Gothic script along the note. The note is printed in black. The note is not dated, the issue date is taken from the Withdrawn Banknotes Reference Guide, issued by the Bank of England.

Reverse: Not printed

Type	Issued	P#	X
O40/1914N[1]	7 August 1914	347	

20.4. O40/1914N² 2ⁿᵈ series Treasury 1 Pound note

Issued a few months after the former on better quality (banknote) paper.

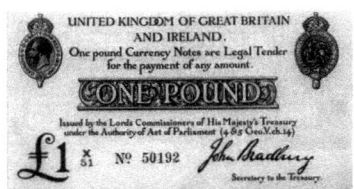

Obverse

Obverse: Vignette of King George V in upper left corner, St. George slaying the dragon in the upper right corner. "ONE POUND" in centre of the note. Printed in black, not dated.

Reverse: Not printed

Type	Issued	P#	X
O40/1914N²	23 October 1914	349	

20.5. O40/1917N 3ʳᵈ series Treasury 1 Pound note

A third series of 1 Pound Treasury notes was issued in 1918. This series lasted longer than the earlier and only stopped being issued after the Bank of England gained the responsibility of issuing banknotes of all values in England.

Obverse

Reverse

Obverse A¹: Vignette of King George V to the right. St. George slaying the dragon to the left. "ONE POUND" in centre of note. Issued for "UNITED KINGDOM OF GREAT BRITAIN AND IRELAND". Printed in brown and green.

Obverse A²: As obverse A¹ but issued for "UNITED KINGDOM OF GREAT BRITAIN AND NORTHERN IRELAND".

Reverse A: Parliament buildings in London.

Type	Issued/Signatures	P#	X
O40/1917NyyyyA¹A	22 January 1917; Bradbury (1917), Warren-Fisher (1919)	351, 357, 359	
O37/1818NyyyyA²A	Warren-Fisher (1927)	361	

20.6. O40/1928N Series A 1 Pound banknote

In 1928 the Bank of England took the responsibility to issue also lower denomination (that is lower than 5 Pounds) banknotes. It is issued in two colour variations, and with or without security thread (in cataloguing this is considered to be part of the obverse).

Obverse A¹

Obverse A²

Obverse A³

Obverse A¹: Vignette of Britannia to the left and "1 POUND" to the right. Issuer and value in the centre of the note. Signature of Chief Cashier in lower left. This note is green. No metal thread.

Obverse A²: As obverse A¹ but colour pale blue and orange. Issued as a wartime emergency issue. Note includes metal thread.

Obverse A³: As obverse A¹ (colour green) with metal tread included.

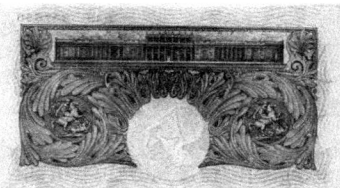

Reverse A¹   *Reverse A²*

Reverse A¹: Ornamental design including building at top and two vignettes showing St. George slaying the dragon. The colour is green.

Reverse A²: As reverse A¹, but colour is pale blue and orange.

Type	Issued/Signatures	P#	X
O40/1928NyyyyA¹A¹	22 November 1928; Mahon (1928), Catterns (1929), Peppiatt (1934)*	363	
O40/1928NyyyyA²A²	29 March 1940; Peppiatt (1940)	367	
O40/1928NyyyyA³A¹	13 September 1948; Peppiatt (1948), Beale (1949), O'Brien (1955)	369	

*The first type was reissued for about three months in 1948 in order to use up pre-war banknote paper.

20.7. O40/1960N Series C 1 Pound banknote

Issued with one design only. The first 1 Pound banknote featuring a portrait of Queen Elizabeth II.

Obverse   *Reverse*

Obverse: Portrait of Queen Elizabeth II to the right, "One Pound" in centre of note. The note is printed in green.

Reverse: Searing Britannia in centre, "ONE POUND" in centre of note. Mostly gray and green.

Type	Issued/Signatures	P#	X
O40/1960Nyyyy	17 March 1960; O'Brien (1960), Hollom (1962), Fforde (1966), Page (1970)	374	

20.8. O40/1978N Series D 1 Pound banknote

Last Pound note before it was replaced by the nickle-brass coin.

Two very slightly different obverse and reverse designs.

Obverse A¹   *Obverse A²*

Obverse A¹: Queen Elizabeth II to the right, green signature.

Obverse A²: As obverse A¹ but black signature.

Reverse A¹   *Reverse A²*

Reverse A¹: Sir Isaac Newton. Guilloches at lower left and right are dark.

Reverse A²: As reverse A¹ but Guilloches are light green.

Type	Issued/Signatures	P#	X
O40/1978NyyyyA¹A¹	9 February 1978; Page (1978)	377a	
O40/1978NyyyyA²A²	20 March 1981; Somerset (1981)	377b	

20.9. O40/1983C Nickel-brass 1 Pound coins (1983-2016)

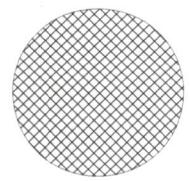

In 1983 the Pound note was replaced by the Pound coin. When it was introduced it was decided that the reverse of the coins would have a different heraldic design each year. The designs would be representative for the United Kingdom as a whole, or of one of the constituting countries, England, Scotland, Wales or Northern Ireland. Apparently originally there were 5 designs that would be repeated every five years, but after two periods different designs were drafted for each of the countries that were used for two periods again. After these four designs representing bridges were used. Only from 2008 a permanent design was introduced in the for of the uncrowned shield of the Royal Armes. It is only after

2008, when more (and different, one year only) designs were issued each year that these different designs are considered commemorative designs and are no longer incorporated in this catalogue. As a result of this a total of 15 reverse designs (5 of which were one year only designs) are recognised compared to only four obverse designs.

| Obverse A | Obverse B | Obverse C¹ |

Obverse A   *Obverse B*   *Obverse C¹*

Obverse C²   *Obverse D*

Obverse A: Second head of Queen Elizabeth II facing right.

Obverse B: Third Head of Queen Elizabeth II facing right.

Obverse C¹: Fourth head of Queen Elizabeth II facing right, with beads along the edge of the coin.

Obverse C²: As obverse C¹ with beads removed.

Obverse D: Fifth head of Queen Elizabeth II facing right.

Reverse A   *Reverse B*   *Reverse C*

Reverse D   *Reverse E*   *Reverse F*

Reverse G   *Reverse H*   *Reverse I*

Reverse J   *Reverse K*   *Reverse L*

Reverse M   *Reverse N*   *Reverse O*

Reverse A: Royal Arms representing the United Kingdom (1983, 1993, 1998, 2003, 2008).

Reverse B: Thistle and royal diadem representing Scotland (1984, 1989).

Reverse C: Leek and royal diadem representing Wales (1985, 1990).

Reverse D: Flax Plant and royal diadem representing Northern Ireland (1986, 1991).

Reverse E: Oak Tree and royal diadem representing England (1987, 1992).

Reverse F: Crowned shield of the Royal Arms representing the United Kingdom (1988).

Reverse G: Lion rampant representing Scotland (1994, 1999).

Reverse H: Dragon passant representing Wales (1995, 2000).

Reverse I: A Celtic Cross with a Pimpernel Flower in the centre surrounded by an ancient Torc representing Northern Ireland (1996, 2001).

Reverse J: Three Lions passant guardant representing England (1997, 2002).

Reverse K: The Forth Railway Bridge representing Scotland (2004).

Reverse L: The Menai Bridge representing Wales (2005).

Reverse M: The Egyptian Arch Railway Bridge representing Northern Ireland (2006).

Reverse N: The Gateshead Millennium Bridge representing England (2007).

Reverse O: Shield of the Royal Arms (2008-2016).

Type	Years	KM#	S#	Y#	X
O40/1983CyyyyAA	1983	933	423		
O40/1983CyyyyAB	1984	934	424		
O40/1983CyyyyBC	1985, 1990	941	431		
O40/1983CyyyyBD	1986, 1991	946	436		
O40/1983CyyyyBE	1987, 1992	948	438		
O450/1983CyyyyBF	1988	954	444		
O40/1983CyyyyBB	1989	959	445		
O40/1983CyyyyBA	1993	964	456		

Type	Years	KM#	S#	Y#	X
O40/1983CyyyyBG	1994	967	459		
O40/1983CyyyyBH	1995	969	461		
O40/1983CyyyyBI	1996	972	464		
O40/1983CyyyyCJ	1997	975	468		
O40/1983CyyyyC¹A	1998, 2003, 2008	993	487		
O40/1983CyyyyC¹G	1999	998	503		
O40/1983CyyyyC¹H	2000	1005	512		
O40/1983CyyyyC¹I	2001	1013	514		
O40/1983CyyyyC¹J	2002	1030	525		
O40/1983CyyyyC¹K	2004	1048	545		
O40/1983CyyyyC¹L	2005	1051	549		
O40/1983CyyyyC¹M	2006	1059	568		
O40/1983CyyyyC¹N	2007	1074	573		
O40/1983CyyyyC²O	2008-2015	1113	600		
O40/1983CyyyyDO	2015-2016				
O40/1983CyyyyZ	2009-....	Commemorative designs			

20.10. O40/2017C Bimetallic 1 Pound coin (2017-....)

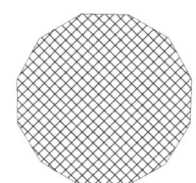

A problem with the nickel-brass 1 Pound coin is that it is one of the most counterfeit coins in the world. It is estimated that about 3% of all 1 Pound coins in circulation are by now counterfeit and for that reason it has been decided to replace the coin. This will be done from 2017 with a 12 sided coin that appears in shape to be comparable to the pre-decimal nickel-brass threepence coin. It will be a bimetallic coin that features as many as possible security characteristics.

Reverse A

Obverse A: Fifth head of Queen Elizabeth II facing right.

Reverse A: Four emblems to represent each of the nations of the United Kingdom – the English rose, the leek for Wales, the Scottish thistle, and the shamrock for Northern Ireland – emerging from a single stem within a crown. The above image is taken from the Royal Mint website and represents the winning reverse design for the new coin.

Type	Years	KM#	S#	Y#	X
O40/2017CyyyyAA	2017-....				

21. O43/ 2 Pounds (GBP 2.00)

Not many 2 Pounds series have been in circulation in the United Kingdom. At about the time of the Great Recoinage paper 2 Pound notes of the Bank of England circulated, and these were to replace by the gold double sovereign coins. Although occasionally gold double sovereigns were minted they never gained widespread circulation, probably due to their large value and most were minted for presentation purposes such as for proof sets. In only four years (1823, 1887, 1893 and 1902) circulation strikes were produced, and even these in quantities which were minute when compared to the gold single sovereign pieces. The double sovereigns are however incorporated here as they were occasionally minted as circulation coins. As such also the early proofs and the modern proofs issued for Quen Elizabeth II are incorporated here, just like the half and single sovereign were incorporated. During the 1990 new nickel-brass 2 Pound coins were introduced for commemorative purposes and since 1997 a bimetallic series of circulation 2 Pounds coins is circulating widely for the first time. This last series also contains, just like the 50 pence series a very large number of commemorative coins that are not individually classified in this catalogue.

Series	Years	Comp.	Mass (g)	Size (mm)	THK (mm)
O43/1797N	1797-1821	Paper		appr. 113x200	
O43/1820C	1820-....	Gold (91.7% Au, 8.3% Cu)	15.98	28.4	1.4
O43/1986C	1986-1996	Nickel-brass (70% Cu, 24.5% Zn, 5.5% Ni)	15.98	28.4	3.0
O43/1997C	1997-....	Bimetellic*	12	28.4	2.5

Outer ring nickel-brass (76% Cu, 20% Zn, 4% Ni), inner disc copper-nickel (75% Cu, 25% Ni).

21.1. O43/1797N White 2 Pounds banknote (1797-1821)

These uniface banknotes had a simple design indicating that the Bank would pay the bearer on demand the sum of 1 Pound. These notes were first issued in 1797 due to shortages in the gold supply. When enough gold Pound coins, sovereigns were minted after the Great Recoinage of 1816 these notes could be withdrawn again. Unlike the more recent banknotes issued since the 20th century white notes were dated.

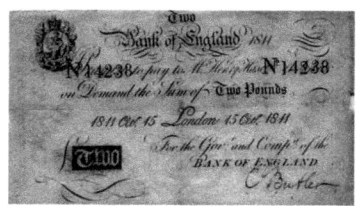

Obverse

Type	Issued/Signatures	P#	X
O43/1797N	2 March 1797; Hase (1807)	191	

21.2. O43/1820C Gold double sovereign (1820-....)

As stated above this coins is, except for a few years, issued for presentation purposes. Only during the reign of Queen Elizabeth II (after 1980) the same obverse design is used for mintages in more than one year. Since 1986 the commemorate 2 Pounds coins are also issued in gold with the double sovereign specifications. These are not individually mentioned herein, but are considered "commemorate designs". Of the regular double sovereigns 14 obverse designs can be recognised and only three reverse designs as most of these coins feature the St. George slaying the dragon reverse.

Obverse B   *Obverse C*   *Obverse D*

Obverse A: Head of King George III facing right.

Obverse B: First head of King George IV facing left. Image from de Bonneville (1849).

Obverse C: Second head of King George IV facing left. Image from de Bonneville (1849).

Obverse D: Head of King William IV facing right. Image

from de Bonneville (1849).

Obverse E: Jubilee head of Queen Victoria facing left.

Obverse F: Veiled head of Queen Victoria facing left.

Obverse G: Head of King Edward VII facing right.

Obverse H: Head of King George V facing left.

Obverse I: Head of King George VI facing left.

Obverse J: First head of Queen Elizabeth II facing right.

Obverse K: Second head of Queen Elizabeth II facing right.

Obverse L: Third head of Queen Elizabeth II facing right.

Obverse M: Fourth head of Queen Elizabeth II facing right.

Obverse N: Fifth head of Queen Elizabeth II facing right.

Reverse A²   *Reverse B*   *Reverse C*

Reverse A[1]: St. George slaying the dragon.

Reverse A[2]: As reverse A[1] with mintage year below. Image from de Bonneville (1849).

Reverse B: Crowned shield of Royal Arms with legend. Image from de Bonneville (1849).

Reverse C: Crowned shield of Royal Arms without legend. Image from de Bonneville (1849).

Type	Years	KM#	S#	Y#	X
O43/1820CyyyyAA[1]	1820	Pn81, Pn82	51a		
O43/1820CyyyyBA[2]	1823	690	73		
O43/1820CyyyyCB	1825-1826	701	74		
O43/1820CyyyyDC	1831	718	88		

Type	Years	KM#	S#	Y#	X
O43/1820CyyyyEA²	1887	768	134	30	
O43/1820CyyyyFA²	1893	786	148	44	
O43/1820CyyyyGA²	1902	806	295	58	
O43/1820CyyyyHA²	1911	821	310	79	
O43/1820CyyyyIA²	1937	860	347	102	
O43/1820CyyyyJA²	1953	Pn137	379		
O43/1820CyyyyKA²	1980-1983	923	409		
O43/1820CyyyyLA²	1984-1993	944	434		
O43/1820CyyyyMA²	1998-2015	1072	493		
O43/1820CyyyyNA²	2015-....				
O43/1820CyyyyZ	Most years since 1986	Commemorative designs			

21.3. O43/1986C Nickel-brass 2 Pounds (1986-1996)

Issued as seven (7) commemorative coins only.

21.4. O43/1997C Bimetallic 2 Pounds (1997-....)

Since 1997 the 2 Pounds coin is a regular circulation coin. It is produced as bimetallic coin lighter and thinner, but with the same diameter, than the former nickel-brass series. The first year of issue there appeared to be problems with the coin flans, as the two parts could separate and for that reason the first coins, although struck in 1997 were only issued in 1998. This caused in the beginning the believe with some members of the public that the coin with the third head of Queen Elizabeth II were very valuable as they were only a small part of the initially issued coins. Since 1999 this coin is issued with at least one commemorative design, in most years even more. Even so, the permanent design has also been issued each year. Unlike other coins from the reign of Queen Elizabeth II this coin saw a change in reverse design when the forth head of the queen was replaced by the fifth head in 2015. This could be done because this coin was part of the general coinage redesign when all other circulating coins in 2008 were given their new obverse design. Except for the numerous commemorative designs this series has seen three obverse and two reverse designs.

Obverse A

Obverse B

Obverse C

Obverse A: Third head of Queen Elizabeth II facing right.

Obverse B: Forth head of Queen Elizabeth II facing right.

Obverse C: Fifth head of Queen Elizabeth II facing right.

Reverse A

Reverse B

Reverse A: Four concentric circles that depicts mankind's industrial and technological progress from the Iron Age to the age of the Internet.

Obverse B: Britannia facing left with trident and shield.

Type	Years	KM#	S#	Y#	X
O43/1997CyyyyAA	1997	976	469		
O43/1997CyyyyBA	1998-2015	994	488		
O43/1997CyyyyCB	2015-....				
O43/1997CyyyyZ	Since 1999	Commemorative designs			

22. O47/ 5 Pounds (GBP 5.00)

The five Pounds denomination is the lowest denomination that has always been used in the form of paper money. Although gold quintuple sovereigns were officially part of the circulation currency in the United Kingdom since 1820 their mintages were always very low, in fact only four issues of them were also minted as circulation strikes in "larger" (that is up to several tens of thousands) mintages.

And since 1990 the large copper-nickel five Pounds coins are issued almost every year, but only as commemorative coins of which circulation is actively discouraged. Even more so, since 2008 these coins are not even produced as circulation strikes anymore. Except for these two coin series the 5 Pounds denomination is issued in the form of five bank note series. Later in 2016 a new, polymer banknote series will be issued.

Series	Years	Comp.	Mass (g)	Size (mm)	THK (mm)
O47/1793N	1793-1955	Paper		133x211 (last issue, earlier smaller at 120x195)	
O47/1820C	1820-....	Gold (91.7% Au, 8.3% Cu)	39.94	36.02	2.2
O47/1957N	1957	Paper		90x158	
O47/1963N	1963	Paper		85x140	
O47/1971N	1971	Paper		78x145	
O47/1990C	1990-....	Copper-nickel (75% Cu, 25% Ni)	28.28	38.61	2.7
O47/1990N	1990	Paper		70x135	
O47/2016N	2016	Polymer		65x125	

22.1. O47/1793N White 5 Pounds banknote (1793-1955)

Like all Bank of England notes issued before World War II (with the exception of the 20th century 10 shillings and 1 Pound banknotes) these uniface banknotes had a simple design indicating that the Bank would pay the bearer on demand the sum of 5 Pounds. Unlike to 1 and 2 Pounds notes these were not withdrawn in 1821/1825 and continued to be in circulation (as the only white note) during and after World War II. The only major anti counterfeiting improvement was the incorporation of a metal security thread in 1945. these notes were last issued in 1957. The size of the notes increased when the metal thread was incorporated from 120x195 mm to 133x211 mm following the information in the Withdrawn Banknotes Reference Guide. The size of earlier/earliest notes was generally a bit smaller.

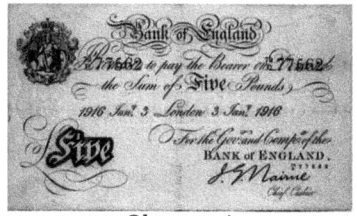

Obverse A   *Obverse B*

Obverse A: 5 Pounds note without metal thread.

Obverse B: 5 Pounds note with metal thread.

These notes are not printed on the reverse.

Type	Issued/Signatures	P# (issues since 1816)	X
O47/1793NyyyyA	Notes are signed and dated between 1793 and 1945. Issued in London or Bank of England branches	192, 210, 221, 232, 241, 250, 259, 268, 277, 286, 295, 304, 312, 320, 328, 335	
O47/1793NyyyyB	Notes are signed and dated between 1944 and 1957, only from London.	342, 343, 344, 345	

22.2. O47/1820C Gold quintuple sovereign (1820-....)

Although coins of 2 and 5 Pounds were part of the legislation related to the Great Recoinage these large coins were only rarely minted for circulation, and if so in mintages that were minute compared to the 1 Pound (sovereign) coins. The very large 5 Pounds coin even more so than the 2 Pounds and this coin was only minted in three years for circulating purposes. It was however minted in small quantities for most monarchs and as such incorporated in the 19th century coin guides. As with the double sovereign coin only after 1980 during the reign of Queen Elizabeth II the coin designs were minted for consecutive years, and special commemorative designs were minted in special years. Of the regular quintuple sovereigns 14 obverse designs can be recognised and only three reverse designs as most of these coins feature the St. George slaying the dragon reverse. The commemorative designs include the various gold versions of the copper-nickel 5 Pounds coins.

Obverse A

Obverse B

Obverse C

Obverse M

Obverse A: Head of King George III facing right. Image from de Bonneville (1849).

Obverse B: Bare head of King George IV facing left. Image from de Bonneville (1849).

Obverse C: Young head of Queen Victoria facing left. Image from Homans & Mushet (1872).

Obverse D: Jubilee head of Queen Victoria facing left.

Obverse E: Veiled head of Queen Victoria facing left.

Obverse F: Head of King Edward VII facing right.

Obverse G: Head of King George V facing left.

Obverse H: Head of King George VI facing left.

Obverse I[1]: First head of Queen Elizabeth II facing right.

Obverse I[2]: As obverse I[1] but "BRITT OMN" removed.

Obverse J: Second head of Queen Elizabeth II facing right.

Obverse K: Third head of Queen Elizabeth II facing right.

Obverse L: So called "uncouped" bust of Queen Elizabeth II facing right. This obverse, in Great Britain unique to the quintuple sovereigns of 1987 and 1988, showed the Queen's shoulders, rather than being cut off at the neck. This effigy was the "normal" effigy for the Isle of Man's commemorative coins between 1985 and 2000.

Obverse M: Fourth head of Queen Elizabeth II facing right.

Obverse N: Fifth head of Queen Elizabeth II facing right.

163

Reverse A¹

Reverse A²

Reverse B

Reverse C

Reverse A¹: St. George slaying the dragon. Image from de Bonneville (1849).

Reverse A²: As reverse A¹ with mintage year below.

Reverse B: Crowned shield of Royal Arms with legend. Image from de Bonneville (1849).

Reverse C: Una and the Lion reverse featuring an image of the Queen before a lion both walking to the right with the date in Roman numerals below. Image from Homans & Mushet (1872).

Type	Years	KM#	S#	Y#	X
O47/1820CyyyyAA¹	1820	Pn83, Pn84	52		
O47/1820CyyyyBB	1826-1829	702	75		
O47/1820CyyyyCC	1839	742	115A		
O47/1820CyyyyDA²	1887	769	135	30	
O47/1820CyyyyEA²	1893	787	149	45	
O47/1820CyyyyFA²	1902	807	296	59	
O47/1820CyyyyGA²	1911	822	311	80	
O47/1820CyyyyHA²	1937	861	348	103	

Type	Years	KM#	S#	Y#	X
O47/1820CyyyyI¹A²	1953	Pn138	380		
O47/1820CyyyyI²A²	1957	*			
O47/1820CyyyyJA²	1980-1984	924	410		
O47/1820CyyyyKA²	1985-1997	945	435		
O47/1820CyyyyLA²	1987-1988	949	439		
O47/1820CyyyyMA²	1998-2015	1003	494		
O47/1820CyyyyNA²	2015-....				
O47/1820CyyyyZ	Many years	Commemorative designs			

*Only mentioned in Lobel (1996).

22.3. O47/1957N Series B 5 Pounds banknote

This is the only banknote that was issued from series B. It replaced the white note which was, due to its simple design, no longer usable due to counterfeiting risks. This note was issued in two versions, with either a black or a white "£5" symbol on the reverse.

Obverse A   *Reverse A¹*

Obverse A: Helmeted Britannia to the left, "FIVE POUNDS" in centre and "£5" in upper and lower right corners.

Reverse A¹: Lion with key. Black "£5" in lower left corner.

Reverse A²: As reverse A¹ but white "£5" in lower left corner.

Type	Issued/Signatures	P#	X
O47/1957NyyyyAA¹	21 February 1957; O'Brien (1957)	371	

Type	Issued/Signatures	P#	X
O47/1957NyyyyAA²	O'Brien (1961)	372	

22.4. O47/1963N Series C 5 Pounds banknote

Issued with one design only. The first 5 Pound banknote featuring a portrait of Queen Elizabeth II.

Obverse   *Reverse*

Obverse: Portrait of Queen Elizabeth II to the right, "Five Pound" in centre of note. The note is printed in blue.

Reverse: Seated Britannia in centre, "FIVE Pounds" above. Mostly printed in blue.

Type	Issued/Signatures	P#	X
O47/1963Nyyyy	21 February 1963; Hollom (1963), Fforde (1966), Page (1970)	375	

22.5. O47/1971N Series D 5 Pounds banknote

Issued with one design. Contains a metal thread of which the width was doubled form 0.5 to 1 mm from 16 July 1987.

Obverse   *Reverse*

Obverse: Queen Elizabeth II to the right.

Reverse: Duke of Ellington (1769-1852).

Type	Issued/Signatures	P#	X
O47/1971Nyyyy	11 November 1971; Page (1971), Somerset (1980), Gill (1988)	378	

22.6. O47/1990C Copper-nickel 5 Pounds coin (1990-....)

Issued as commemorative coins only. After 2008 no circulation strikes were made any more, and as a result new designs are no longer available at face value.

22.7. O47/1990N Series E 5 Pounds banknote

Issued with one obverse and two distinctively different reverse designs. "£5" symbols on obverse changed colour in 1993 and was changed to a much clearer font at the change of the reverse. These notes are predominantly printed in turquoise-blue.

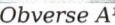

Obverse A¹

Obverse A²

Obverse A³

Obverse A¹: Head of Queen Elizabeth II at right, light "£5" in upper left corner. Crown in upper right corner.

Obverse A²: As obverse A¹ with dark "£5" symbol.

Obverse A³: As obverse A¹ with much bolder, sans serif "£5" symbol at upper left and "5" at upper right corner.

Reverse A

Reverse B

Reverse A: George Stephenson (1781-1848) at right.

Reverse B: Elizabeth Fry (1780-1845) at right.

Type	Issued/Signatures	P#	X
O47/1990NyyyyA¹A	7 June 1990; Gill (1990), Kentfield (1991)	382	
O47/1990NyyyyA²A	1 March 1993; Kentfield (1993), Lowther (1999)	385	
O47/1990NyyyyA³B	21 March 2002; Lowther (2002), Bailey (2003), Salmon (2011), Cleland (2014)	392	

22.8. O47/2016N Polymer 5 Pounds banknote

In 2016 the 5 Pounds banknote will be replaced by a polymer version. The reason behind this change is that polymer notes are cleaner, more secure, and more durable than paper notes, and they will provide enhanced counterfeit resilience and increase the quality of notes in circulation. These notes will be slightly smaller than the Series E 5 Pounds banknotes. A concept of the reverse was published by the Bank of England.

Concept of the reverse of the 2016 Polymer 5 Pounds Banknote

Type	Issued/Signatures	P#	X
O47/2016Nyyyy	(not issued yet when this catalogue was written)		

23. O50/ 10 Pounds (GBP 10.00)

Regular denomination that has only been issued as banknotes. Due to massive counterfeiting by Nazi Germany during World War II the white notes were taken out of circulation in 1943. Only in 1964 new 10 Pounds notes were introduced. Four banknote series have been issued until now (white, C, D and E). A new polymer series will be introduced in 2017.

Series	Years	Comp.	Mass (g)	Size (mm)	THK (mm)
O50/1759N	1759-1943	Paper		133x211	
O50/1964N	1964	Paper		93x150	
O50/1975N	1975	Paper		85x151	
O50/1992N	1992	Paper		75x142	
O50/2017N	2017	Polymer		69x132	

23.1. O50/1759N White 10 Pounds note (1759-1943)

White 10 Pounds banknotes were issued until 1943. During World War II Nazi Germany counterfeited British banknotes (Operation Bernhard) on a massive scale in the hope to destroy, or at least damage, the British economy. When the British government discovered this large scale forgery of banknotes it decided that all notes above £5 would be withdrawn form circulation. They ceased to be legal tender on 16 April 1945. These notes varied slightly over time, but they continued to be recognisable very clearly as the same type of note, hence their classification as only one series and type.

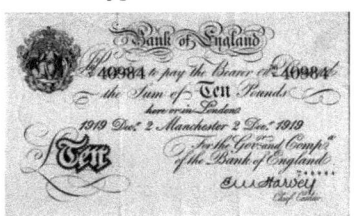

Obverse

Type	Issued/Signatures	P# (issues since 1816)	X
O50/1759Nyyyy	Notes are signed and dated between 1759 and 1943. Issued in London or Bank of England branches	193, 211, 222, 234, 242, 252, 260, 269, 278, 287, 296, 305, 313, 321, 329, 336	

23.2. O50/1964N Series C 10 Pounds banknote

First 10 Pounds note after almost 20 years doing without. Due to inflation the purchasing value of the Pound decreased slowly and the need for higher valued banknotes arose during the 1960s. Issued with one design only. The first 10 Pounds banknote featuring a portrait of

Queen Elizabeth II.

Obverse   *Reverse*

Obverse: Portrait of Queen Elizabeth II to the right, "TEN Pounds" in centre of note. The note is printed in brown.

Reverse: Lion holding key walking to the left. Banner with "TEN POUNDS" in its mouth. The reverse is also is printed in brown.

Type	Issued/Signatures	P#	X
O50/1964Nyyyy	21 February 1964; Hollom (1964), Fforde (1966), Page (1970)	376	

23.3. O50/1975N Series D 10 Pounds banknote

Issued with one design. Contains a metal thread. A new 'windowed' security thread was introduced on 16 July 1987.

Obverse   *Reverse*

Obverse: Queen Elizabeth II to the right.

Reverse: Florence Nightingale (1820-1910).

Type	Issued/Signatures	P#	X
O50/1975Nyyyy	20 February 1975; Page (1975), Somerset (1980), Gill (1988), Kentfield (1991)	379	

23.4. O50/1992N Series E 10 Pounds banknote

Issued with one obverse and two distinctively different reverse designs. Extra "£10" symbols added on both obverse and reverse in 1993 and was changed to a much clearer font at the change of the reverse. These notes are predominantly printed in orange-brown.

Obverse A¹

Obverse A²

Obverse A³

Obverse A¹: Head of Queen Elizabeth II at right, "£10" in upper left corner. Crown in upper right corner.

Obverse A²: As obverse A¹ with "£10" also in upper right corner.

Obverse A³: As obverse A¹ with much bolder, sans serif "£10" symbol at upper left and "10" at upper right corner.

Reverse A¹

Reverse A²

Reverse B

Reverse A¹: Charles Dickens (1812-1870) at right. No "£10" in upper right corner.

Reverse A²: As reverse A¹, "£10" also in upper right corner.

Reverse B: Charles Darwin (1809-1882) at right.

Type	Issued/Signatures	P#	X
O50/1992NyyyyA¹A¹	29 April 1992; Kentfield (1992)	383	
O50/1992NyyyyA²A²	22 November 1993; Kentfield (1993), Lowther (1999)	386	
O50/1992NyyyyA³B	7 November 2000; Lowther (2000), Bailey (2003), Salmon (2011), Cleland (2014)	389	

23.5. O47/2017N Polymer 10 Pounds banknote

In 2017 the 10 Pounds banknote will be replaced by a polymer version. The reason behind this change is that polymer notes are cleaner, more secure, and more durable than paper notes, and they will provide enhanced counterfeit resilience and increase the quality of notes in circulation. These notes will be slightly smaller than the Series E 10 Pounds banknotes. A concept of the reverse was published by the Bank of England.

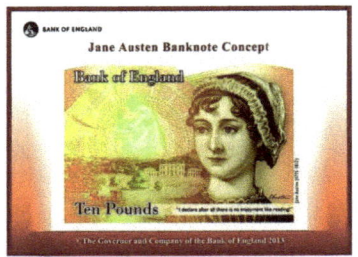

Concept of the reverse of the
2017 Polymer 10 Pounds
Banknote

Type	Issued/Signatures	P#	X
O50/2017Nyyyy	(not issued yet when this catalogue was written)		

24. O52/ 15 Pounds (GBP 15.00)

During the early 19th century several banknotes with "irregular" denominations were issued. At various times these banknotes were discontinued. The 15 Pounds banknote for example already in 1822. This denomination was only issued as "white note".

Series	Years	Comp.	Mass (g)	Size (mm)	THK (mm)
O52/1759N	1759-1822	Paper		127x203	

24.1. O52/1759N White 15 Pounds banknote (1759-1822)

Last issued in 1822. This denomination was considered not longer useful between the 10 and 20 Pounds notes.

Obverse

Type	Issued/Signatures	P# (issues since 1816)	X
O52/1759Nyyyy	Notes are signed and dated between 1759 and 1822.	194	

25. O53/ 20 Pounds (GBP 20.00)

Regular denomination that has only been issued as banknotes. Due to massive counterfeiting by Nazi Germany during World War II the white notes were taken out of circulation in 1943. Only in 1970 new 20 Pounds notes were introduced. Four banknote series can be recognised (white, D, E and F).

Series	Years	Comp.	Mass (g)	Size (mm)	THK (mm)
O53/1725N	1725-1943	Paper		133x211	
O53/1970N	1970	Paper		90x160	
O53/1991N	1991	Paper		80x149	
O53/2007N	2007	Paper		80x149	

25.1. O53/1725N White 20 Pounds note (1725-1943)

White 20 Pounds banknotes were issued until 1943, and withdrawn from circulation due to "Operation Bernhard" They ceased to be legal tender on 16 April 1945. These notes varied slightly over time, but they continued to be recognisable very clearly as the same type of note, hence their classification as one series/type.

Obverse

Type	Issued/Signatures	P# (issues since 1816)	X
O53/1725Nyyyy	Notes are signed and dated between 1725 and 1943. Issued in London or Bank of England branches	195, 212, 223, 234, 243, 252, 261, 270, 279, 288, 297, 306, 314, 322, 330, 337	

25.2. O53/1970N Series D 20 Pounds banknote

First 20 Pounds banknote after 25 years without. Continued inflation made the need for a larger denomination note necessary. Issued with one design. Contains a metal thread. A new 'windowed' security thread was introduced on 15 November 1984.

Obverse   *Reverse*

Obverse: Queen Elizabeth II to the right.

Reverse: William Shakespeare (1564-1626).

Type	Issued/Signatures	P#	X
O53/1970Nyyyy	9 July 1970; Fforde (1970a), Page (1970b), Somerset (1980), Gill (1988), Kentfield (1991)	3809	

25.3. O53/1991N Series E 20 Pounds banknote

Issued with one obverse and two distinctively different reverse designs. The "£20" symbol on the obverse was changed to a much clearer font at the change of the reverse. These notes are predominantly printed in mauve-purple.

Reverse A¹

Reverse A²

Reverse A³

Obverse A¹: Head of Queen Elizabeth II at right, "£20" in upper left corner. Crown in upper right corner.

Obverse A²: As obverse A¹ with "£20" also in upper right corner.

Obverse A³: As obverse A¹ with much bolder, sans serif "£20" symbol at upper left and "20" at upper right corner.

Reverse A²

Reverse B

Reverse A¹: Michael Faraday (1791-1867) at right.

Reverse A²: As reverse A¹ with value "£20" added at top right.

Reverse B: Sir Edward Elgar (1857-1934) at right.

Type	Issued/Signatures	P#	X
O53/1991NyyyyA¹A¹	5 June 1991; Gill (1991), Kentfield (1992)	383	
O53/1991NyyyyA²A²	27 September 1993; Kentfield (1993), Lowther (1999)	386	
O53/1991NyyyyA³B	22 June 1999; Lowther (1999), Bailey (2003), Salmon (2011), Cleland (2014)	389	

25.4. O53/2007N Series F 20 Pounds banknote

Issued since 2007 in only one design.

Obverse   *Reverse*

Obverse: Queen Elizabeth II at right.

Reverse: Adam Smith (1723-1790).

Type	Issued/Signatures	P#	X
O53/2007Nyyyy	13 March 2007; Bailey (2007), Salmon (2011), Cleland (2014)		

26. O54/ 25 Pounds (GBP 25.00)

During the early 19th century several banknotes with "irregular" denominations were issued. At various times these banknotes were discontinued. The 25 Pounds banknote for example already in 1822. This denomination is only issued as "white note".

Series	Years	Comp.	Mass (g)	Size (mm)	THK (mm)
O54/1765N	1765-1822	Paper		127x203	

26.1. O54/1765N White 25 Pounds banknote (1765-1822)

Last issued in 1822. This denomination was considered not longer useful with its value close to 20 Pounds.

Obverse

Type	Issued/Signatures	P# (issues since 1816)	X
O54/1765Nyyyy	Notes are signed and dated between 1765 and 1822.	196	

27. O55/ 30 Pounds (GBP 30.00)

During the early 19th century several banknotes with "irregular" denominations were issued. At various times these banknotes were discontinued. The 30 Pounds banknote for example in 1852. This denomination is only issued as "white note".

Series	Years	Comp.	Mass (g)	Size (mm)	THK (mm)
O55/1725N	1725-1852	Paper		130x211	

27.1. O55/1725N White 30 Pounds banknote (1725-1852)

Last issued in 1852.

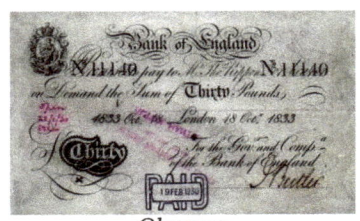

Obverse

Type	Issued/Signatures	P# (issues since 1816)	X
O55/1725Nyyyy	Notes are signed and dated between 1725 and 1852.	197, 213, 224	

28. O56/ 40 Pounds (GBP 40.00)

During the early 19th century several banknotes with "irregular" denominations were issued. At various times these banknotes were discontinued. The 40 Pounds banknote for example in 1851. This denomination is only issued as "white note".

Series	Years	Comp.	Mass (g)	Size (mm)	THK (mm)
O56/1725N	1725-1851	Paper		130x211	

28.1. O56/1725N White 40 Pounds banknote (1725-1851)

Last issued in 1851.

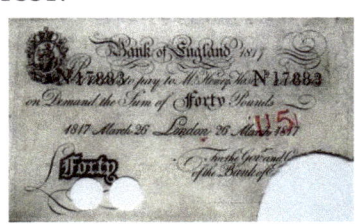

Obverse

Type	Issued/Signatures	P# (issues since 1816)	X
O56/1725Nyyyy	Notes are signed and dated between 1725 and 1851.	198, 214, 225	

29. O57/ 50 Pounds (GBP 50.00)

Regular banknote that continued to be in circulation until massive counterfeiting by Nazi Germany during World War II forced the government to take them out of circulation in 1943. Only in 1981 new 50 Pounds notes were introduced. Four banknote series can be recognised (white, D, E and F). Not a very popular note. During the period I lived in the United Kingdom from 1994 until 1998 I never saw any of them in "daily" live. At this moment it is the largest denomination Pounds banknote in circulation. As larger purchases are more and more made electronically it is not expected that even larger denomination banknotes are reintroduced in the near future.

Series	Years	Comp.	Mass (g)	Size (mm)	THK (mm)
O57/1725N	1725-1943	Paper		133x211	
O57/1981N	1981	Paper		95x196	
O57/1994N	1994	Paper		85x156	
O57/2011N	2011	Paper		85x156	

29.1. O57/1725N White 50 Pounds note (1725-1943)

White 50 Pounds banknotes were issued until 1943, and withdrawn from circulation due to "Operation Bernhard" They ceased to be legal tender on 16 April 1945. These notes varied slightly over time, but they continued to be recognisable very clearly as the same type of note, hence their classification as one series/type.

Obverse

Type	Issued/Signatures	P# (issues since 1816)	X
O57/1725Nyyyy	Notes are signed and dated between 1725 and 1943. Issued in London or Bank of England branches	199, 215, 226, 235, 244, 253, 262, 271, 280, 289, 298, 307, 315, 323, 331, 338	

29.2. O57/1981N Series D 50 Pounds banknote

Introduced in 1981 as it was expected that there was demand for an even larger denomination than 20 Pounds. In spite of continued inflation it never became a note that saw large general circulation. Issued with one design. Contains a metal thread. A new 'windowed' security thread was introduced on 21 July 1988.

Obverse

Reverse

Obverse: Queen Elizabeth II to the right.

Reverse: Sir Christopher Wren (1632-1725).

Type	Issued/Signatures	P#	X
O57/1981Nyyyy	20 March 1981; Somerset (1980), Gill (1988), Kentfield	3809	

Type	Issued/Signatures	P#	X
	(1991)		

29.3. O57/1994N Series E 50 Pounds banknote

Unlike the other series E banknotes issued with one design only, clearly illustrating the continued lack of general circulation of this denomination. These notes are predominantly printed in red.

Obverse   *Reverse*

Obverse: Head of Queen Elizabeth II at right, "£50" in upper left and right corners.

Reverse: Sir John Houblon (1652-1712) at right.

Type	Issued/Signatures	P#	X
O57/1994Nyyyy	20 April 1994; Kentfield (1992), Lowther (1999), Bailey (2003),	388	

29.4. O57/2011N Series F 50 Pounds banknote

Issued since 2011.

Obverse   *Reverse*

Obverse: Head of Queen Elizabeth II at right.

Reverse: Portraits of Matthew Boulton (1728-1809) and James Watt (1736-1819).

Type	Issued/Signatures	P#	X
O57/2011Nyyyy	2 November 2011; Salmon (2011), Cleland 2014		

30. O60/ 100 Pounds (GBP 100.00)

Only issued as white notes until these were withdrawn from circulation in 1943.

Series	Years	Comp.	Mass (g)	Size (mm)	THK (mm)
O60/1725N	1725-1943	Paper		133x211	

30.1. O60/1725N White 100 Pounds note (1725-1943)

Issued until 1943, and withdrawn from circulation due to "Operation Bernhard", and ceased to be legal tender on 16 April 1945.

Obverse

Type	Issued/Signatures	P# (issues since 1816)	X
O60/1725Nyyyy	Notes are signed and dated between 1725 and 1943. Issued in London or Bank of England branches	200, 216, 227, 236, 245, 254, 263, 272, 281, 290, 299, 308, 316, 324, 332, 339	

31. O63/ 200 Pounds (GBP 200.00)

Only issued as white notes. They were last issued in 1928.

Series	Years	Comp.	Mass (g)	Size (mm)	THK (mm)
O63/1725N	1725-1928	Paper		133x211	

31.1. O63/1725N White 200 Pounds note (1725-1928)

Issued until 1928. Still in circulation in 1943 thus withdrawn due to "Operation Bernhard". They ceased to be legal tender on 16 April 1945.

Obverse

Type	Issued/Signatures	P# (issues since 1816)	X
O63/1725Nyyyy	Notes are signed and dated between 1725 and 1928. Issued in London only.	201, 217, 228, 237, 246, 255, 264, 273, 282, 291, 300, 309, 317, 325	

32. O65/ 300 Pounds (GBP 300.00)

Only issued as white notes. They were last issued in 1855, according to the Bank of England. According to Pick (1980) they were issued until 1885. I however consider the Bank of England as the authority in this and stay with their "last issued" date.

Series	Years	Comp.	Mass (g)	Size (mm)	THK (mm)
O65/1725N	1725-1855	Paper		130x211	

32.1. O65/1725N White 300 Pounds note (1725-1855)

Only issued as white notes. Issued until 1855.

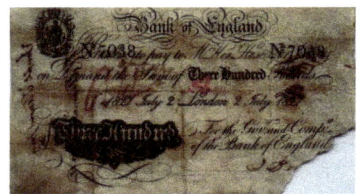

Obverse

Type	Issued/Signatures	P# (issues since 1816)	X
O65/1725Nyyyy	Notes are signed and dated between 1725 and 1928. Issued in London only.	202, 218, 229, 238, 247, 256, 265, 274, 283, 292	

33. O67/ 500 Pounds (GBP 500.00)

Only issued as white notes. They were last issued in 1943.

Series	Years	Comp.	Mass (g)	Size (mm)	THK (mm)
O67/1725N	1725-1943	Paper		133x211	

33.1. O67/1725N White 500 Pounds note (1725-1943)

Issued until 1943 and withdrawn due to "Operation Bernhard". They ceased to be legal tender on 16 April 1945.

Obverse

Type	Issued/Signatures	P# (issues since 1816)	X
O67/1725Nyyyy	Notes are signed and dated between 1725 and 1928. Issued in London or Bank of England branches	203, 219, 230, 239, 248, 257, 266, 275, 284, 293, 301, 310, 318, 326, 333, 340	

34. O70/ 1000 Pounds (GBP 1000.00)

Only issued as white notes. They were last issued in 1943.

Series	Years	Comp.	Mass (g)	Size (mm)	THK (mm)
O70/1725N	1725-1943	Paper		133x211	

34.1. O70/1725N White 1000 Pounds note (1725-1943)

Issued until 1943 and withdrawn due to "Operation Bernhard". They ceased to be legal tender on 16 April 1945.

Obverse

Type	Issued/Signatures	P# (issues since 1816)	X
O67/1725Nyyyy	Notes are signed and dated between 1725 and 1928. Issued in London only except for Hull between 1882 and 1889.	204, 220, 231, 240, 249, 258, 267, 276, 285, 294, 302, 311, 319, 327, 334, 341	

35. P00/ 1,000,000 Pounds (GBP 1,000,000.00)

In Scotland (3) and Northern Ireland (4) a total of seven private banks have the right to issue banknotes of their own. These banknotes needs to be backed for the overwhelming part by physical Bank of England banknotes. As backing the Bank of England issues large denomination banknotes of one million and one hundred million Pounds. These notes are used only internally within the Bank and are never seen in circulation. They are based on the old white note designs and printed in red. The One Million Pounds note, which are nicknamed "Titans", are A5 in size. Images of these notes are published by the Bank of England in an album on their Flickr photo sharing profile (https://www.flickr.com/photos/bankofengland/albums/721 57640347497784). The Bank of England preferred that these images were not reproduced here, and for that reason the interested reader is referred to the images published on Flickr. As can be seen on these images these notes are not dated, but their issue date can be estimated from the signature of the Chief cashier.

36. P20/ 100 million Pounds (GBP 100,000,000.00)

The 100 Million Pounds banknotes (Giants) are issued for the same reason as the One Million Pounds banknotes. They are, like the million Pounds banknote also printed in red and are A4 in size. Images of a 100 million Pounds banknote are also published by the Bank of England in an album on their Flickr photo sharing profile (https://www.flickr.com/photos/bankofengland/albums/721 57640347497784). As with the one million Pounds notes the Bank of England preferred that these images were not reproduced in this publication, and for that reason the interested reader is referred to the images published on Flickr. As can be seen on these images these notes are not dated, but their issue date can be estimated from the signature of the Chief cashier.

Literature

Bank of England (2016) Withdrawn Banknotes Reference Guide. Find information on banknotes issued by the Bank of England and HM Treasury since 1694. Available from the Bank of England: http://www.bankofengland.co.uk/BANKNOTES/Pages/deno m_guide/default.aspx

Bonneville A (1849) Encyclopédie monétaire ou nouveau traité des monnaies d'or et d'argent en circualtion chez les divers peuples du monde. Chez l'auteur, Paris. Available from Google Books: https://books.google.nl/books?id=krMQAQAAMAAJ

Christmas H (1864) The copper and billon coinage of the British Empire. Available from Google Books: https://books.google.nl/books?id=nY4TAAAAQAAJ

Couby M (1986) The British bronze penny from 1860 to

189

1970. Available from http://www.michaelcoins.co.uk/

Couby M (2005) The British bronze coinage 1860-1869. 4th edition. Available from http://www.michaelcoins.co.uk/

Christmas H (1864) The copper and billon coinage of the British Empire. Available from Google Books: https://books.google.nl/books?id=nY4TAAAAQAAJ

Cuhaj GS (2010) Standard catalog of world paper money. Volume 3. Modern issues 1961-date. 16th edition. Krause Publications Inc, Iola, WI.

Davies PJ (1982) British Silver Coins since 1816.

Freeman M (1985, reprint 2006) The Bronze Coinage of Great Britain, 2nd edition. Spink, London.

Homans IS & Mushet R (1872) The coin book, comprising a history of coinage. JB Lippingcott & Co., Philadelphia. Available from Google Books: https://books.google.nl/books?id=IH0aAAAAYAAJ

Krause CL & Mishler C (1998) 1999 standard catalog of World coins. 26th edition. Krause Publications, Inc, Iola, WI.

Krause CL & Mishler C (1999) Standard catalog of World coins. 1801-1900. 2nd edition. Krause Publications, Inc, Iola, WI.

Lobel R, Davidson M, Hailstone A & Calligas E (1996) Coincraft's standard catalogue of English & UK coins 1066 to date.

Marles RJ (1998) Collectors coins Great Britain. 25th edition. Rotographic Publications.

Marsh MA (2002) The gold sovereign. Golden Jubilee edition. Cambridge (Publications).

Marsh MA (2004) The gold half-sovereign. 2nd edition. Cambridge (Publications).

Peck, CW (1958) English copper, tin and bronze coins in the British Museum 1558-1958).

Perkins CH (2006) Collectors' bank notes, treasury and Bank of England. 14th edition. Rotographic.

Perkins CH (2014) Collectors' coins GB. Pre-decimal issues 1797-1970, 40th edition. Rotographic.

Perkins CH (2014) Collectors' coins. Decimal issues of the United Kingdom 1968-2014. Rotographic.

Pick A (1980) Standard Catalog of World Paper Money. 3rd edition. Krause Publishers.

Rayner PA (1992; reprint) English silver coinage since 1649. London.

Schön G & Kahn H (2014) Weltmünzkatalog 19. Jahrhundert. Battenberg verlag.

Schön G & Schön G (2014) Welmunzkatalog 20. & 21. Jahrhundert. 42. Aulage. Battenberg Verlag.

Shafer N & Cuhaj GS (2003) Standard catalog of world paper money. Volume 3. Modern issues 1961-date. Krause Publications Inc, Iola, WI.

Spink (1999) Standard catalogue of British coins; Coins of England and the United Kingdom. 34th edition.

Yeoman RS (2008) A catalog of modern World coins 1850-1964. 14th edition. Whitman Publishing LLC, Atlanta GA.

www.ingramcontent.com/pod-product-compliance
Lightning Source LLC
Chambersburg PA
CBHW051147120626
46547CB00012B/984

* 9 7 8 9 0 8 1 6 0 5 9 8 4 *